A Universal Passion

MUSIC AND DANCE FROM MANY CULTURES

Monica Connell

For Alphonse

with love and thanks

Monica x

A Universal Passion

MUSIC AND DANCE FROM MANY CULTURES

Monica Connell

redcliffe

First published in 2008 by Redcliffe Press Ltd.,
81G Pembroke Road, Bristol BS8 3EA

© Text and photographs, Monica Connell, 2008

The author and publishers thank Arts Council England
for supporting this project.

ISBN 978 1 904537 86 1

British Library Cataloguing in Publication Data:
A catalogue record for this book is available from the British Library

Design and typesetting by E&P Design, Bath
Printed and bound in the UK by The Charlesworth Group, Wakefield

Contents

ACKNOWLEDGEMENTS

I am very grateful to the following people: Myra Connell who read each section of the manuscript as it was finished and always responded with enthusiasm, encouragement, and helpful suggestions; Ursula Monn for introducing me to African music and dance in this area and being my 'artistic partner'; Siobhan Kierans who generously shared all she knows; Peter Higgs who hand printed the photos with 'mood and passion' and helped me to edit them; Adrian Mitchell who supported, encouraged, nurtured and shared my obsession with the book on a daily basis.

I would also like to thank: John Sansom and all at Redcliffe Press; June Burrough and the Pierian Centre; Lorraine Ayensu, Peter Netley, Deasy Bamford, Emma Flatley, Tribe of Doris, Steve Elloway and Alan Cossey.

Above all I am indebted to the arists who generously shared their lives with me. This book is for them and for all the talented musicians and dancers in this country who, because of cultural and ethnic differences, remain unrecognised.

All photographs were taken on a Nikon FM2 camera, using Fuji 800 film. All are from original hand prints by Peter Higgs at Argent 2, in Bath.

A Universal Passion was supported and made possible by the Arts Council of England.

Introduction

For the last five years I have been photographing musicians and dancers at festivals and community events. My favourite working position is as close to the stage as I can get and, to avoid distracting the audience, off centre to the left or right depending on the direction of the light. This means that I'm often within feet of the musicians and dancers. From here, following the movement with my camera, working with the rhythm and music and waiting for that split second in which to take my photograph, I almost feel part of the performance. Sometimes one of the musicians will look at me and smile or play to the camera and sometimes I catch myself swaying to the music, oblivious to the consequences of camera shake.

This position of intimacy has taught me amongst other things that music is a language. Musicians talk to each other through music, dancers through movement, musicians and dancers interrelate through rhythm, and every performance is a conversation with the audience. It is a language that speaks to the heart and body as well as the head, and whose currency is enjoyment. But most importantly it is a language that is spontaneous and universal, that communicates between cultures without translation or learning of verbs. As Chartwell Dutiro says (page 54), 'Music is a bridge between cultures. It is the only way I know of transcending that stereotype of them and us.'

Every summer as I stand in front of the stage at Bristol Harbour Festival or Refugee Week's Big Fun Day, where the performers are from many cultures and the audience is a cross section of the local community, I feel moved and thrilled to see people from such diverse backgrounds united by music. While the performance lasts, issues of racism, injustice, the residual antagonisms of our shared history, are put aside as people who may never have reason or opportunity to speak to one another, clap, sing, dance or simply enjoy the music together.

But what happens when the music stops?

Personally I wanted to know more about the performers from different parts of the world. I wanted to meet them and ask about their art. I wanted to put their music and dance in the context of its country of origin. I wanted to know what opportunities there are to perform in this country, whether there's a demand to learn the music and dances of other cultures, whether these traditions are passed from generation to generation within their culture of origin or whether, in an inhospitable environment, they wither and die.

There are of course many indigenous musicians and dancers, who never achieve the recognition their talent deserves. For non-indigenous performers the chances of 'making it' are infinitely slimmer, not only because of potential difficulties with language and bureaucracy, but because of the prejudice and cultural arrogance of would-be promoters. This was pointed out to me by Cyrus Khajavi (page 41) who suggested that although we have a multi-million pound world music industry in this country the music and musicians selected for promotion are those that 'fit the Western person's holiday-snap image of what Africa or Asia should be.' And I was truly ashamed when Louis Roger Eboa (page 33) said, 'I don't want to sound rude but in this country, in the context of dance, African dancers are second-class citizens'.

A Universal Passion is an attempt to introduce musicians and dancers from diverse cultures to an audience they might not necessarily meet through their art. Its inspiration is the exhilaration I felt as I photographed them; exhilaration generated by the music and dance *per se* but also by the way these united so many cultures in a mood that was generally one of exuberance and joy.

—

Before I go any further I feel that I should introduce myself. If promoters of world music can show prejudice and cultural arrogance, what about photographers and editors of books about 'world' musicians and dancers? It's easy to get defensive and say, 'Of course I'm not prejudiced', but where does conscious prejudice end and unconscious preconception begin? Certainly we can deal with and eradicate what's conscious but what about the unconscious preconceptions that are part of our culture and conditioning? These are camouflaged and slippery, insidiously informing everything all of us do and think with ideas about things we know nothing about. I try constantly to rid myself of these but the question is how do you learn to think purely as an individual and not as a product of your background? Is it even possible?

It would be convenient to say that in this book the performers introduce themselves directly through interviews and photographs. But that's not true. Much of it – for example the selection of performers, the photographs chosen, the questions in the interviews, the editing – is mediated by me (and presumably the 'baggage' of my preconceptions). So the best I can do is to make clear who I am and how I arrived at some of the decisions that helped shape the book.

I'm a white woman. I was born in England and brought up in Northern Ireland, in Belfast. My mother was German, my father Irish. I have a degree in sociology and a postgraduate diploma in social anthropology. I have lived for two years in a remote village in the Jumla region of north-western Nepal doing anthropological fieldwork, and on the basis of this I have written a book called *Against a Peacock Sky* (Viking, 1991). I now live in Bristol and work as a photographer. To my constant regret, I am neither a musician nor a dancer.

—

All the performers featured in the book live in the vicinity of Bristol – three in Devon, three in or close to Bath, one in Cardiff, and the rest in Bristol itself. This geographical requirement means that I've had to exclude many talented artists whose performances I have photographed at local events but who don't live in the area. If I'd reached further the book would have become unwieldy and I wanted to keep the focus tight: I wanted to portray a particular area at a particular moment in time.

Beyond this, my selection is driven by photographs. As I explained above, the inspiration for the book is the shared exuberance generated by the performance, so I wasn't prepared to stage any of the photos in a studio. If I had, the mood would have been lost. This means that to an extent the musicians and dancers were pre-selected for me by the organisers of community events (so for example I wasn't able to search for artists who aren't yet established enough in this country to perform in public – for which I'm sorry).

The pre-eminence of photographs created another limitation. Dance photography (and to a lesser extent music photography) is notoriously difficult: often the stages or marquees where I photographed were poorly lit and the dancers, sometimes in groups, were moving incredibly fast in directions that were hard to predict. A lot of the photos were simply out of focus – and not in a pleasing way. Others were spoiled by things like a dancer moving her arm in front of her face or one dancer moving in front of another. Dance is about movement, flowing, and you only have to look at photographs of yourself dancing at parties to know how utterly ridiculous dancers (and this includes professional ones) can look frozen in time. So there are one or two artists I would have liked to include (for example Mamadou Cissokho, a Senegalese kora player) but the pictures I took of them just weren't good enough.

Within these criteria I have selected performers from countries with as wide a geographical span as possible (including Europe, South America, Africa, India, Tibet and the Caribbean). Most of the artists were born in the countries whose music and dance they perform, but I chose several who were born here or elsewhere because I was interested in how cultural heritage is transmitted (or in some cases revived) within the UK.

Qualifications, training, commercial success and public renown were not requirements. They are not what the book is about.

—

I would prefer to let each interview speak for itself rather than attempting an overview or analysis, but there are a few trends I'd like to point out.

All the performers are passionate about their art forms and pursue them with burning commitment, often in the face of adversity. Many have become professional performers against the wishes of their parents and families, who often see music and dance as careers which are either culturally unrespectable or unworthy of them. Cyrus Khajavi's father (Iran) was horrified that his son wanted to be an 'entertainer' and pressed him (unsuccessfully) to train as an architect or an engineer. Dr Joel (India) bowed to his father's wishes that he become a doctor, but when he'd reached a senior position at the World Health Organisation he gave it all up because he couldn't bear life without music. Louis Roger Eboa (Cameroon) describes how he struggled against bullying, victimisation, and his parents' disapproval to become a dancer in a country where men should be macho, men who dance professionally are seen to be gay, and being gay is a crime.

For many of the women there are the added pressures and expectations of motherhood. Rachel de Garang (Sudan) didn't dance for ten years when her children were young because her husband didn't approve of it. Claudia Aurora left Portugal to escape her parents' expectation that she become an office worker or get married and have children. Eugenia Ledesma (Argentina) who is a single mother battled for years to pursue her music and dance despite working full time and providing a home, care and love for her son. She compares her own situation to that of her father who is also a musician and dancer: 'In terms of commitment I learned a lot from my father. He wasn't committed to many things but he was certainly committed to his art. Maybe he was more selfish than I think I am – but he was also brave. You can be like that as a woman – a mother – but you have to be twice as determined and push twice as hard – and there's sacrifice.'

Almost all the artists feel a strong desire to teach their art. Bi Do Irie: 'It's important to me when I learn something new that I share my knowledge and don't keep it all to myself...' According to Alphonse Daudet Touna 'culture is for sharing'. For some of the artists this almost amounts to an obligation based on the belief that there is something in their art that we in Britain and people everywhere would benefit from learning. Dr Joel likens himself to a missionary for South Indian *konnakol*, or vocal percussion, which he feels 'can help anyone compose, perform, or appreciate the rhythm of any music in the world...and should be part of the general musical education everywhere'. Chartwell Dutiro also compares himself to a missionary for mbira, which he feels can guide us towards our spirituality. Chartwell emphasises this idea of obligation when he says that he didn't *choose* to come to England and make a life out of mbira, he was 'called' to do it by the ancestors.

Sometimes I wonder whether Bristol and the South West are particularly well endowed with musicians and dancers from diverse cultures, or whether that impression reflects the number of multicultural events at which the public can see them perform. The photographs were taken at the following events: St Paul's Carnival, Bristol Asian Festival, Exiles Express, Big Fun Day (which is part of Bristol Refugee Week), Bristol Harbour Festival, Ashton Court Festival, Sounds of Afrika Festival in Devon, and Tribe of Doris Intercultural Summer School also in Devon (see page 100).

Certainly there *are* a lot of events at which multicultural music and dance are brought to public awareness. But it's also true to say that these events encourage musicians and dancers to settle in this area as opposed to other parts of the UK. And then a kind of snowballing effect takes place whereby the more musicians and dancers who live in this area the more who want to live here because it gets to be known that there's a good world music/dance 'scene'... with its contingent opportunities for employment and companionship.

Tribe of Doris has been particularly instrumental in this process. I've lost count of the number of musicians and dancers who told me that Tribe of Doris was the reason they came to Bristol or the South West, that it was at Tribe of Doris that they had their first opportunity to teach in this country, that it was at Tribe of Doris that they met other musicians and dancers with whom they now perform. For so many international musicians and dancers who, for whatever reason, find themselves in this country – perhaps alienated, lonely, and disconnected from their art – Tribe of Doris is like 'family'.

—

Tribe of Doris Intercultural Summer School takes place for five days every year in a three-field site near Taunton in Devon. Although everyone camps and the music and dance take place in marquees or in the open air, it distinguishes itself from a festival in that it's based around workshops where international musicians and dancers (some of whom live in the UK and some of whom come here for the occasion) are booked as teachers and everyone else is a 'participant' or student.

The *organisation* Tribe of Doris – Siobhan Kierans and Deasy Bamford, who founded the Summer School in 1991 and the Tribe of Doris 'team' – is based in Bristol. Here it co-hosts with Refugee Action and Bristol City Council's Refugee and Asylum Services (led by the musician Lorraine Ayensu) an annual one-day event as part of International Refugee Week. Like the Summer School, Big Fun Day aims to promote understanding and respect between cultures primarily through music and dance.

A Universal Passion owes a lot to Tribe of Doris. Seven of the photos were taken at the Summer School and fifteen of the performers were introduced to me by Siobhan Kierans. I'm convinced that it was because of our mutual Tribe of Doris connections that all of these artists were enthusiastic about the book and welcomed me into their lives like a friend.

—

The interviews took place between February and December 2007. Most of them lasted for about an hour and all were recorded. To some extent they were structured, in that there were certain subjects I wanted most of the artists to at least touch upon – these included childhood, a description of their art, how they learned it, how it relates to the wider culture in its country of origin, how and where they practise it here and their plans for the future. So before each interview I researched (as best I could) the relevant country and art form and devised some appropriate questions; but most of the time I became so engrossed in what the artist was telling me that I never once looked at the question sheet.

The transcripts ranged from ten to seventeen pages and because I wanted the final versions to be concise, much of our conversation had to be lost. Often it was bewilderingly difficult to find a path through the maze of experiences, emotions and thoughts. My guidelines were the themes above – which constitute the under-current of the book. But I also wanted to reflect the uniqueness of each person's experience and prevent the book from becoming repetitive, so if the editing chose to go off at a tangent, that's often what happened.

I've kept the conversational tone of the interviews not only to make them more immediate but because the sound of a person's voice, their delivery and the rhythm of their speech say as much about the person's character as their actual words. Conversational language has its own rules of pacing, musicality, punctuation and grammar – all of which I have tried to retain. For many of the artists English is a second, third or even fourth language and while I loved listening to the idiosyncrasies this gives rise to, and feel that these reflect the artist's experiences, I decided – not to *correct* them because in the context of conversation who am I to say what's right and what's wrong – but to smooth some of them out.

Although the interviews as they appear in the book are in fact paraphrases (or a series of quotes woven together by me in what I hope is the 'voice' of the artist) I use the first person because so many of the performers told me that they feel 'marginalised' and don't have a 'voice' in our society and I didn't want to exacerbate this further by writing for example, 'He/she was born in...' I justified this decision by showing the reworked interview to each of the artists. Most of them immediately approved, a few asked me to change certain things, and in the end everyone was happy.

—

The year in which the interviews were carried out, 2007, was the bicentenary of the abolition of the slave trade on which Bristol's past and continuing prosperity was partly founded. There were a lot of commemorative events in the city and a certain amount of discussion and controversy, which were inevitably 'in the air' (if not actually mentioned) in some of the interviews. Ayodele Scott whose forbears were slaves suggests that we all (black and white) use this opportunity to think about those times and find a way in which we can all work together to 'redeem the spirit of our shared history'.

Working on the book has taught me three principles about music and dance: they are a universal language that unites cultures; they are border anarchists, putting down roots and cross-fertilising wherever they go; they are irrepressible. African drumming and dancing spread with the slaves from Africa, and on their journey (a journey which still goes on) enhanced many cultures and spawned innumerable cross-mutations from jazz, to soul, to reggae, to break-dance, to the catch-all 'fusion'. The music of the mbira was banned in Zimbabwe by British missionaries who labelled it 'music of the devil' – but now here it is in the country of the very people who banned it, being taught and played to us by Chartwell Dutiro, because he feels that it can help us access our spirituality. What an irony! And what great generosity of spirit!

As most of the artists in the book know and Tribe of Doris and many other organisers of community events know – and I have only just found out – music and dance play a fundamental role in establishing a racially, ethnically and culturally harmonious future.

—

A *Universal Passion* has been a long journey. I have met some truly remarkable people and through their eyes I have visited much of the world. I have also been inspired, educated, uplifted and moved not only by their music and dance but by our friendship and the conversations we have had. I feel indebted to them all and I hope that this book does justice to their talent, commitment and the vibrancy they bring to our society.

MONICA CONNELL
April 2008

Bi Do Irie

IVORY COAST

Some people here look at Africans and they think, 'Oh yes, you were born in Africa, you can dance, you can drum'. But it's not true. There are many people in Africa who can't sing, can't drum, can't dance. Maybe when you're little and your mum is getting food for you and food for herself she'll be happy and she will sing and dance and try to give you rhythm. But when you grow up, if you don't take that further, you won't become a musician. I loved music. I loved dancing. So I gave myself power to learn.

Yes, in the village there was drumming all around me. If someone was sick we would drum for the spirits so they could tell us why he was sick and what we could do about it. If there was a good harvest, people would drum and dance to celebrate. If people were happy – simple – they would drum and dance. But in the village we have respect for the generations, so when you're young you don't play drums – you stand there and listen. And then someone might say, 'You. Come and try this'. So you go and try and if you have talent, one day one of the drummers might say, 'Oh so and so can't drum tonight, but there's a little boy called… Bi Do,' and someone would come and fetch me. Because I was the youngest I couldn't do anything that would seem pushy or disrespectful, but if I was *called* to drum, that made me happy… *really* happy.

When I left school I went to Abidjan to look for a job. I couldn't find anything at first but then I met a friend who was driving taxis and he told me that he'd driven a woman to the city centre and when she got out of the taxi she'd said, 'If you have any brothers or sisters who can dance, send them along to my school.' So he took me there and the next thing I knew was that I had a free place at the Marie Rose Guiraud School to be trained in traditional singing, dancing, drumming and choreography.

At first I found it really difficult. There are sixty-three tribes in Ivory Coast and they all have different cultures, different languages, different songs, different dances – and we had to learn everything. But I am someone who likes difficulty. I like to learn and I like to push myself. Maybe it's because my mother died when I was six and from then on I knew that I was alone and if I didn't do things for myself, no one else would do them for me. I was with the school for ten years. For the first four years I was learning and after that I started to perform. We toured all over the world – Japan, America, Europe…

It's important to me when I learn something new that I share my knowledge and don't keep it all to myself, so I went to Germany to teach African drumming, dancing and singing. I also started a band. It was called Zavoalo. Everyone in it was from Ivory Coast and we played traditional music. We had three different drums *djembe, atougblan* – which is a tall drum that stands on the floor and you play with a stick – and talking drum. We also had shakers, me singing and four dancers.

I like living in different countries because as well as teaching people about my own culture, I can learn about theirs. So I lived in Germany for ten years and then I moved to England. I now teach more than I perform and sometimes I think that's what I prefer. There's so much to learn in a drum – if you're a beginner you can have a good experience but if you learn to play really well you can be the happiest person in the world. If your brain is free and you're relaxed, whatever you want to talk about, you can play that on a drum.

I moved from London to Bristol because of my children. I was afraid that when they grew up they'd get into trouble. Children don't have a good life here. In Africa we have a community and within the community people look after each other. If you're a child your grandparents can show you different trees and plants and say, 'Oh this one can do this and this one can do that'. It's the same for farming and drumming. But here what are old people going to teach their grandchildren? Sometimes, if I go out at night and there are children around, I'm afraid they'll get hurt. But children are our future – all of our futures. And whether we're parents or not we're all responsible.

When I first came to England I was really happy because there are so many people from different countries. It's like a garden with every flower you can think of. But English people never move… they never really experience other cultures. Part of the reason I'm here is to learn about your culture and I'd like to take all of my good students to my village so they can learn about mine. I'd divide them up and put each person with a different family and teach them, not just drumming and dancing, but how my people live. I invite you to come to my village and learn…

JULY '07

Photograph: Tribe of Doris, 2007

Sonia Mumtaz

BANGLADESH/UK

When my sister Mumtaz and I were growing up in Bristol we used to dress up in Indian costumes – one of us as a man, the other as a woman – and we'd put on a Bollywood video and dance and sing the parts of the actors. No one ever taught us Bollywood dancing – we just learned from watching the films.

Every day when we arrived at school all we talked about was Bollywood: What were you and your family watching last night? Have you seen *Qayamat se Qayaman Tak* or *Tezaab* (or whatever the latest film happened to be)? Isn't Salman Khan *gorgeous*? Sometimes at the end of the year a group of us would get together and rehearse a Bollywood dance that we'd perform in front of the school. Bollywood represented a fantasy world of glamour and glitz and romance and my sister and I and most of our friends were in love with it.

Bollywood dancing is rooted in classical Indian dances such as Bharata Natyam and Kathak, which in their early forms were practised in temples by *devadasis* or temple dancers, as an act of worship. Later the maharajas employed *devadasis* as courtesans to dance for their private enjoyment. Gradually, as dancing lost its association with worship and became a form of entertainment, it

started to be popular at weddings and parties and eventually in Bollywood films. Bollywood today is a combination of classical Indian dance with salsa, rock and roll, modern jazz, bellydancing, breakdancing… every kind of dance rolled into one in a flamboyant mixture of glitter and colour.

When I was seventeen a friend of mine, Koldeep, told me that Channel 4 was looking for potential Bollywood actors to audition for a programme called 'Bollywood Star'. It was to be a four-part series based around the search for a British Bollywood actor who would be sent to Mumbai, which is the centre of the Bollywood film industry, to be trained for a role in a film. At first I thought, 'No…I'm not going to do that', but Koldeep insisted and soon after I'd applied, Channel 4 contacted me say that they wanted to come and film me dancing. I couldn't believe it when they used my film to introduce the programme. Every week as soon as it started there I was dancing on national television.

In the end I made it to the final twenty out of about a thousand applicants. I was disappointed not to win because I'd come so close – but the experience gave me confidence. I started to do solo performances and people would tell me how much they enjoyed watching me because I looked so happy when I was dancing. I still get nervous – sometimes when you're out there and you know you've made a mistake you think everybody's watching you, but you have to let it go and focus on each moment, because there's only two or three minutes to enjoy yourself before the song is over. And the following day you're on such a high…

Soon after 'Bollywood Star' Mumtaz and I decided to form a dance company, Bollywood Glamour. Both of us choreograph and perform and Mumtaz is in charge of designing and making the costumes and jewellery. We usually perform to a song from the Bollywood chart which is well known to most of the audience, and the choreography tells the story of the song. The costumes are also based around the song – sometimes it calls for a traditional Indian look with saris and bare feet and sometimes Mumtaz designs our costumes around trainers and jeans. But whatever else we wear we always have glitter and shimmer and sparkle.

We both also teach individual students and groups. People come to our classes for all sorts of reasons – some want to connect to their heritage maybe three or four generations back, some love the costumes and jewellery, some want to get fit, some want to improve their confidence. Two or three years ago most of our students used to be Asian but recently Bollywood has become much more mainstream and we teach people from all over the world. But whatever the reason for learning, students always enjoy themselves – dressing up, singing along as they dance like Bollywood actors do, expressing the emotions of the song with eye movements, body language and hand gestures – because Bollywood is fun.

When I was a teenager Mumtaz and I went to Bangladesh. We wanted to see where our family had come from and where Mumtaz had been born. We didn't mean to go for long but in the end we stayed for three years, living with our grandparents and setting up a beauty business, where we did quite well with hair do's and make-up and decorating Asian brides. I loved it in Bangladesh but I wanted to continue my studies so in the end we came back.

I'm not sure what the future will hold for me. At the moment, as well as performing and teaching, I have a job with local radio, and I'd also like to use my degree, which is in Business and Media. But whatever career I end up doing, Bollywood will always be my hobby and my passion – and sometimes, when I look back at the days when Mumtaz and I used to dance in front of the TV, I realise how much we owe our mother, Azara Mumtaz, and our brother, Murad Fayyaz, for encouraging us and giving us the confidence to become what we always dreamed we would be – Bollywood dancers.

DECEMBER '07
*Interviewed with the kind help of Gulshanara Mumtaz
(usually known as Mumtaz) and Gerdine Wright*
Photograph: Bristol Asian Festival, 2007

Cecilia Ndhlovu
ZIMBABWE

We used to dance under the trees. We had really tall gum trees in my school and in the afternoon we would go into the shade to dance and drum. They were traditional dances of the Ndebele people – *mantshomani*, *isitshikisha* and gumboot dance. Sometimes we spent all day making our costumes – necklaces from seeds that fell from the gum trees, skirts from rice sacks that we collected in the industrial area and cut into shreds, and headdresses from chicken feathers that we brought from our homes.

Those dances came to me from nowhere. Sometimes the teachers would ask my mother if a spirit came to someone in our family and if we danced at home for the ancestors. She said no. But sometimes our neighbours and other people had a big gathering and danced for the ancestors and I'd go over there on my own and dance with them until two or three in the morning. My mother used to get really angry and say that I wasn't supposed to be there. But even when I was eight years old she could hardly drag me away.

One day a dance troupe called Black Umfolofi came to our school looking for female dancers to go with them to Spain. I was one of the dancers they chose. My mother thought it was some sort of dream and I was so over-excited I hardly remember a thing. And

when I was a bit older I went to stay with my sister in Harare. I knew someone there who played with Oliver Mtukudzi and she said, 'We're playing in this hotel tonight, why don't you come along?' I ended up gate-crashing on stage, playing conga, and afterwards Oliver said to my friend, 'Who is she? Where is she from? Can she come to my studio on Monday?' I thought my friend was joking. When I went to his studio he was recording his album *Izayinaovo* and I ended up singing backing vocals. My family didn't even believe me until the album came out and they saw my photograph and my name in the credits.

I sang with the band for eight years. We toured all over the world – America, Canada, Germany, Belgium, France, England. In Zimbabwe a lot of people would point to me in the street and say, 'She sings with Oliver Mtukudzi!'

But things were getting tough in Zimbabwe. When I grew up everything was so beautiful – we had a good life. Now there is nothing but fighting and chaos. People are dying needlessly all over the country and there are shortages of food and petrol and medication. If you are a musician and try to tell the truth about what's happening, things can get really dangerous.

In 1999 Oliver recorded an album called *Bvuma*, which means tolerance. There was a song on it where an old man is told to take things easy and rest, and the government thought it was a call for President Mugabe to retire. One night when we were playing in Harare the police came in with tear gas and destroyed the show and the next morning the album was confiscated from all the shops and bars and clubs and banned on the radio.

I remember my last day with the band. We had just come back from America and we were doing a big show in the stadium. I was wearing a T-shirt that said Bvuma, from the new album. Afterwards when I was driving home with my brother and sister we were stopped by the police. They saw my T-shirt and said, 'You're the one who sings with Oliver Mtukudzi!' I was taken to the police station and questioned for hours and they slapped me to make me say what they wanted to hear, which was that the song was about the president. But Oliver is an artist – I don't know why he wrote the song.

After that things got really bad. Oliver has been taken several times. But he is such a big star – if anything happened to him there would be an international outcry and anyway those big guys can pay their way out. But someone like me could just disappear… and no one would ever know.

I came over here on my own. At first I didn't know anyone and I wasn't doing any music or dancing – I was just studying. Then one year I went to Tribe of Doris and I met so many other musicians and dancers from Africa and all over the world. After that I started to sing and drum again and I began to teach gumboot dance which I'd learned as a child. It started in the mines in South Africa where my forefathers were taken to work. They worked for the white people and they weren't allowed to communicate so they started to tap out a rhythm with their boots and all of a sudden this became a dance as well. At first it was only done by men, but now women do it too.

Sometimes I get very lonely – like when I'm ill – and I just wish I could be with someone. Sometimes I have this dream that I'm at home with my mum and then when I wake up in the morning I feel so sad to be alone. The drumming and dancing help a lot – they keep my mind occupied. If I wasn't doing them… I don't know. But until this president goes and we can go home, we just have to live with it.

MAY '07

Photograph: Bristol Refugee Week, 2007

Alain Hernandez Cuni

CUBA

When I was five years old my father left our family and my mother said to me, 'You're the eldest, you're the man of the family, you have to look after your brothers and sisters'. So when my mother was at work my granny and I cooked and cleaned and took care of my four brothers and sisters. My father didn't send us any money so when I was seven or eight, I used to help people go to the market and I gave whatever money I earned to the family. Even when I was a teenager I didn't resent it – I just accepted that I always had to think ahead about what was happening at home.

I learned to dance at school – salsa, rumba, mambo, danzoń cha-chachá, Mozambiqué, pilón – traditional Cuban dances, Afro-Cuban dances and all those elegant European-influenced dances that they used to do in the salons. When I was five years old I won a prize for dancing, and when I was a bit older our teacher chose me amongst some of the best dancers from different schools to join her company. We used to rehearse after school and we performed at festivals in Havana and once or twice in Pinar del Rio, in the west.

I grew up next to a religious house. My grandfather is a *babalawo*, one of the highest officiants in the Santería religion, which is the

Yoruba religion that was brought to Cuba by African slaves who worked on the sugar plantations. Every day, when the Santeros were practising for their ceremonies, the house would be filled with drumming and dancing and singing and I always felt really drawn to it. But Santería is different from other religions in that you aren't necessarily born into it and you can't decide to become a Santero, you have to wait for the Orishas, the gods and goddesses, to choose you. So I thought, 'If it's my path to follow this, so be it...'

And then strange things started to take place. I could be walking down the street and someone would stop me and say, 'I know you don't know me but the Orishas have given me this message for you.' And they'd talk to me for about an hour, telling me all about my life and what was going to happen to me, and instead of going forwards my life started to stand still and even go backwards. I consulted all sorts of people, religious people, a Tarot reader... and everything pointed in the same direction. So one by one I took the Santero vows, I received some of the Orishas and eventually, after four or five years, when I knew that was what I really wanted to do, I initiated.

To communicate with the Orishas, to bring them down so we can honour and respect them and ask for their guidance, we drum, we dance and we sing. There's a different dance for each Orisha – Ellegua is a child so you dance like a child, Obbatala is the god of peace so you wear nothing but white, and Chango is the god of thunder so you dance like a thunderbolt. Sometimes when I'm dancing I feel different gods next to me, my energy changes, my face changes...

When I first came to England I didn't want to have anything to do with dance. I'd been working as a chef in Havana so I carried on with that. But sometimes my wife Laura and I would go dancing at salsa places, and the salsa we saw here was nothing like the salsa we knew in Cuba. So I decided to run salsa classes with a friend from Havana. Several years later I was asked to teach Orisha dances at Tribe of Doris and next week I'm starting in Bristol.

One of the first things I say to my Orishas students is, 'This Afro-Cuban dancing is not for parties. As soon as we beat a drum or dance or sing, we're calling the Orishas to come down. It's spiritual music.' Sometimes when I'm teaching, the Orishas will pass through the room and touch people. You know when it's happening because you can feel something spinning that starts in your feet and moves up to your head. It's like a trance. The singing and the music are so beautiful and the feeling goes right to your heart.

A lot of people in England are spiritual. They're not religious in a formal sense but they know there is something there. My job as a Santero is to communicate with those people and bring them together. Sometimes I look at the way my life has been shaped by having to look after my brothers and sisters, and I'm grateful. At one time I was studying economics, learning to play saxophone, working to support my family and dancing as well – and it was just too much. So I gave up economics. But I love living in Bristol, and I love teaching Orishas – and I know that if I had an economics degree I couldn't have left Cuba.

OCTOBER '07

Photograph: Tribe of Doris, 2007

Louis Roger Eboa
CAMEROON

I always knew that I was going to be a dancer. I knew that I was going to come to Europe and I knew that I would travel around the world with my dance. When I was a child, wherever I happened to be, as soon as the music started, I had to dance. And in the evenings when the other boys were playing football, all I wanted to do was dance. In Africa it's not good for a boy to dance. If you dance you're not a boy, you're a boy-girl, you're a gay boy. People used to point at me and call me names and my father would say, 'Go to school! Become an accountant.' But I knew I could never be an accountant.

When I was seventeen I left school and joined a professional dance company. At first we did mainly traditional dance. People used to hire us to perform at weddings and other events. In Cameroon there are special dances for weddings, births, christenings and funerals and, although we could improvise a little, we had to make sure we had the right dance for the right event. Our main duty was to make people happy, so we would do a bit of our own choreography first, which would be fun and flamboyant and modern, and then we would do a very traditional piece that everyone knew and could join in. If people didn't join in we weren't considered successful.

Later we did more of our own work and became quite well known. Often artists from Europe would come to our company looking for dancers and our manager would say, 'Oh Louis, Louis can dance' – so I got to work with a lot of different companies and choreographers. Suddenly I was appearing on TV and everywhere. I became quite famous in Cameroon.

One day I lied to my father so badly... I was asked by this woman to dance on a video clip and at first I said no – because my father didn't allow me to dance – but she begged me. So in the middle of the night when my father was sleeping I escaped through my sister's window. A few days later my father was drinking in the bar, and the barman who was watching TV started clapping and said, 'Excuse me, Sir, isn't that your son?' My father looked up and there I was dancing on this huge screen – and my father thought, 'Wow!' Everyone congratulated him and told him what a great dancer I was. That night my father asked me why I'd lied to him and I just said, 'Because I had to'. From that day on, every time I wanted to go dancing my father just said, 'Go'.

Like all Cameroonians I was desperate to go to Paris. People would say, 'Oh, yes, in Paris they dance in the streets – *and* they get paid for it!' I was so excited when this woman who was taking her own company to perform there asked me to join them. But I had a bad experience. First of all at the airport I was taken for a police check and they told me my passport was fake. They held me for hours, and when they eventually let me through I thought, 'OK, this is just the airport'. But things were no better in the city. I was so disappointed. So I came to England – first London, then Bristol. I work on my own now, for different companies. Sometimes I do a performance in London for a few weeks or months – but I always come back to Bristol. I also teach African dance to adults and school kids.

Coming to Europe made life easier for me. In some African countries there's freedom of sexuality, just like there's freedom of religion. But in Cameroon being gay is a crime. I could have stayed and tried to prove to my family that I was straight – got married, had children. But if I'd made that mistake, I'd be so unhappy – how could I dance? I love my family and when I got married I was determined to build a way for them to accept my partner. So I phoned my mother (my father had passed away by then) and said, 'I'm coming to Cameroon – but I'm not coming alone.' 'Who are you coming with?' 'I'm coming with my partner, you know, the one I married six months ago.' 'You're coming here with a *man*?' I was expecting shouting, screaming, crying – but no it was laughter, happiness, hugging. I was so grateful for that.

I'm very happy performing and teaching as I do at the moment but like all dancers I'd love to do more choreography, and I'd love – love – to have my own African Dance Company which could put both feet on the ground here in Bristol and say, 'Yes, we are an African Dance Company and our choreographer is Louis Roger Eboa'. One day I know it will happen. One day…

JUNE '07
Photograph: Bristol Harbour Festival, 2006

Shelok Tsering
TIBET/INDIA

My mother died when I was really young and my father had no way of caring for me so I was sent to an orphanage school in Dharamsala at the age of five. My father took three of us to the school, my two sisters and myself, but the little one, Phurbu Bhutti, was only two at the time and my father said it would have broken his heart to leave her there, so he took her home and my uncle looked after her in the daytime while my father went to work.

I grew up with no memory at all of my parents. The next time I saw my father, when I was about thirteen, was like meeting him for the first time. He told me that he had been one of eleven brothers, but when the Chinese invaded Tibet only two of them managed to escape. He has never talked much about his suffering but I imagine that in 1959 when the Chinese came in with guns and tanks and started killing people, my father, who was still a child, was one of the lucky ones who escaped to India with his Holiness the 14th Dalai Lama. He and his one brother were granted political refugee status by the Indian government and settled in Kalimpong, in west Bengal. My other nine uncles were possibly amongst the million or so Tibetans who were killed.

The school I went to, the Tibetan Children's Village School in Dharamsala, was founded by the mother of his Holiness – and it taught me everything. One of the subjects we did every day was History of Tibet and we learned all about our culture and what had happened to our country and our people and why it's important that we carry on the struggle and never forget. And then once a year all the children worked together on this huge History of Tibet project which included singing and dancing competitions and making models of the Potala, which is the palace of his Holiness in Lhasa, and of our people in their traditional costumes.

Singing is one of the gifts from my school. When I first came to England in 1994, I went to see the Norwegian lady who sponsored my education and she showed me a school report she had received when I was about eight. It said, 'Shelok never concentrates on her studies but she always loves singing'.

Singing is part of the Tibetan way of life – or it used to be. There were wedding songs, change of season songs, peace songs, good wishes songs, songs that people sang when they were building a house or farming – and the nomads, when they were herding their yaks with the whole open space just for themselves, they would sing so loud that their voices echoed in the mountains and were carried by the wind, and then maybe another nomad who was herding sheep or yaks somewhere in the distance would hear their song and sing back.

Singing is also part of religious festivals – and many of the instruments played by the monks and yogis in their sacred rituals and public festivals are the same ones used in traditional folk music. There is, for example, a drum called *nga,* which can be huge or so tiny that you can hold it between your thumb and forefinger; *peewah,* a kind of fiddle; *yangche* which is like a metal xylophone. People used to walk miles from all over the country to go to those festivals just to feel the presence of the monks and Rinpoches, and to see them performing their masked dances and singing and chanting.

Sometimes here in England I perform with a friend, Phuntsok, who plays *dra nye,* which is a bit like a guitar, but most of the time I prefer to sing solo. My voice is very soft and doesn't project, which can sound quite pleasing, but if I sing with music it's easy to feel that my voice is being drowned. I often sing emotional songs about what has happened to my country and how my people have suffered and I like to think that my message is heard.

So many people in this country have never heard of Tibet and I'm afraid that if we don't take care of our people and our culture and history, Tibet will be like an endangered species that is becoming extinct. So my husband, Dawa, and I teach in schools and run workshops – about our history, about Buddhism, about our singing and dancing, about the food we eat – and if every person we share our culture with passes that knowledge on, then slowly, slowly...

To be able to sing in your own language and tradition is a beautiful thing. I hope I can carry on with that. As to whether Tibet will ever be free – it's been fifty years since the Chinese invaded. In terms of one person's life that's a very long time but in terms of history it's nothing. I just hope we can stick to our path of non violence – because it's difficult to draw attention to our situation without bombing and killing, and there are a lot of young people who are getting very frustrated. But if we free Tibet with non-violence it will be a good result for everyone and will give us all hope for world peace. I think Tibet will be free – we just have to hope for that – maybe not in our generation but... things are changing.

AUGUST '07

Photograph: Big Fun Day, Bristol Refugee Week, 2007

Cyrus Khajavi

IRAN

I grew up in a small town in the mountains in the Khorasan province of north-eastern Iran. It was a very colourful area – both culturally and musically. There were Kurds, like my father, and there were Azerbaijanis and Turkomans – all with their own language and culture and brightly coloured costumes. And there was so much music – any excuse and people would get out the *sorna*, which is a wind instrument, a bit like an oboe, and there were big round drums that you beat with drumsticks.

In our own house too people were always singing or banging on something or other. My mother was from Azerbaijan and she and her sister would sing folk songs and lullabies in their own language. My mother also played a kind of accordion. She wasn't very good – but we all humoured her and said, 'Oh that's lovely' and she laughed because she knew she wasn't great. But she had a beautiful singing voice.

When I was a teenager my family moved to Mashhad, which is the second biggest city in Iran. I was just old enough to catch bits of what was happening in the sixties and I fell in love with western rock music. The Beatles, Jimi Hendrix… God! It seemed to capture everything I wanted to say, to feel, to experience.

My father had big plans for me. He had always encouraged me to sing at family gatherings and was really proud of the fact that I had a good voice but when I said I wanted to be a musician, it was panic stations, 'No son of mine's going to be an entertainer!' So I was sent to England to train as an architect or an engineer – both of which earned big money in Iran.

I arrived in January and it was so cold and grey. I went to Bath first because I had some contacts there, but soon afterwards I moved to Bristol where I signed up at a language school. It was a depressing time... never before or since have I experienced loneliness like that, but then I met this Irish guy, Brian – an amazing guitarist. We moved into a squat and spent our time playing guitar. We were so dedicated – it was the most important thing in both of our lives.

As I became more experienced I started to play with bands. I moved to London and joined a rock band called Quasar which seemed to be going places. I stayed with them for six years and just when we were getting to be really well known – we were about to tour Europe – I decided I didn't want to play this music any more. It was really complicated rock music, with pyrotechnics and we wore make up and leathers – and I just wanted to be rid of all that and get down to the core of it.

For a while – and really just for the money – I played for Iranian pop musicians. This was soon after the Revolution and a lot of established musicians had fled Iran because their music and the songs they were singing were considered over-influenced by the West and decadent. These were big stars playing at the Albert Hall and places. I didn't enjoy this time, but one good thing came out of it. I became friends with one of the singers, Toofan, and together with an Iranian classical violinist, Farzad Khavand, we formed a band. We played a lot of gigs together but after two years the band folded. Then in 1990 I started another band. That was Kooch.

Kooch today is a three-piece band – guitar, violin and cello – with me singing. Its roots are partly in Western rock music and partly in the traditions of my childhood. I write most of the lyrics myself and they're in Farsi. We also sing some of my mother's Azerbaijani folk songs, but with our own musical arrangement.

Kooch is very special to me. I'd like it to be bigger and I'd like it to be full time. But it's frustrating... we get good reviews, good feedback, but we don't get booked for any of the big world music festivals because the organisers say we don't fit in. I sometimes feel that the world music industry in this country is biased towards a certain type of music and musician that fits the western person's holiday snap image of what Africa or Asia should be – and that if I grew a beard and performed wearing a turban and baggy colourful trousers things would be different.

A while ago I went to Iran to get our music licensed to be sold in shops and broadcast on TV – and that was hilarious! All music in Iran has to be approved by the Ministry of Culture, so after weeks of waiting, I finally got an appointment with the panel of judges. When I went to their office one of them said, 'So you want to be a singer?' I said, 'I already am a singer – I've brought a CD.' 'If you're a singer, sing!' It was nine o'clock in the morning, I had no guitar, I was getting increasingly angry – but I decided to go for it.

I passed that test but the next one – to get my lyrics approved – I failed. I had written a song called 'Rain'. In it I talk about rain bringing the promise of a place where red, blue, yellow – beautiful colours – are free from the tyranny of blackness. I suppose they thought it was about Iran and the tyranny of the clerics over creativity and freedom of speech.

So I feel that I'm trapped – between one set of expectations in Iran and a different set here in England. Maybe I'm cutting off my nose to spite my face – but I'm proud of the fact that I can stand up and say, 'This is Cyrus – I've lived some of my life in Iran, some of it in England, I've been a rock musician and this is what comes out of it now – this is Kooch.'

JULY '07

Photograph: Exiles Express, Kuumba Centre, 2005

Eugenia Ledesma

ARGENTINA

When I was eight or nine my father started his own dance company and he and a friend of his – Mario García, who was quite a famous dancer – trained me and my younger brother in Argentinian folk dancing. We were still at school at the time but in the evenings and at weekends we used to perform with my father's company. I danced with them and later I drummed – congas and bongos.

We did all sorts of traditional dances. *Malambo* is a man's dance. It's a very showy dance, the dance of the *gaucho*. There's a lot of footwork and you configure it with your poncho or with a *flacon*, which is a kind of sword they use in the countryside. Samba – Argentinian samba – is a courtship dance where you do little figures – *vuelta entera* and *media vuelta* – with your partner and there's a lot of skirt work and hand work, clicking fingers – a bit like flamenco but not as choppy. And polka… where the woman starts the dance, improvising and showing herself off for about five or ten minutes and then the man comes in with his little bit of *malambo*, and then they both dance together.

I used to wear Latin things – tiered skirts and half-moon tops with a frill around them and the boys wore the *bombacha* – you know the *gaucho* thing, with the bobbly trousers and boots and belts with lots of coins. And we all, boys and girls, wore *vinchas* – the scarf that you wrap across your forehead and tie at the back. That's from the Indian people.

There's a lot of Indian influence in Argentinian dance, especially from the north, which is where my father came from. In the north there's still a strong indigenous population, whereas in Buenos Aires and the Pampas in the south the Indians were persecuted and a huge number were killed. You notice the Indian influence in the lyrics too, which speak of oppression and the poverty and inequality we have in our country.

I loved being part of my father's dance company. But when my parents split up all that came to an end. I hardly saw my father for a long time and it was years before I danced again professionally.

I came to England when I was nineteen – my Argentinian husband was doing a postgraduate course in Reading. For a while I worked in shops and catering and then I did an English proficiency course, trained as a secretary, and got a job in an office. But I never really fitted in, so I started working as a life model at Bower Ashton Art College. I loved Art College so much that I decided to do a degree in fine art.

It was during my second year that I met Andy Sheppard, the saxophonist, and rediscovered music. I began to drum again, I joined the Bristol Samba School where I drummed and danced. I learned salsa. I sang with different bands – salsa, samba and Spanish rumba. My son Marcos was also born at that time. I was a single mother, a student and I was rediscovering music and dance, so it wasn't easy for him. I was a good mother I think – but the son of an artist is a hard thing to be! In terms of commitment I learned a lot from my father. He wasn't committed to many things but he was certainly committed to his art. Maybe he was more selfish than I think I am – but he was also brave. You can be like that as a woman – a mother – but you have to be twice as determined and push twice as hard. And there's sacrifice…

For years I drummed and sang with different bands – Latin music, rumba, salsa, *son cubano*, reggae, fusion. I went on tour, I recorded – but I was too busy to rehearse all the time and there was very little money. So I taught salsa and *merengue* and drumming and singing.

Salsa came to me easily because the step is like the step of the Argentinian *chacarera* – except that with salsa you put a bit more into your hips. I teach adults, school children, I teach movement for healing for disabled people. I also have a community job in an after-school club – where I do everything with the kids from dancing and percussion to cooking, cleaning and fundraising.

Marcos is now 22 and I've come to a point where I've been thinking about all the things that I've done, and the fragmentation I sometimes feel inside. I need to give up my community job and focus on my passion for music and dance. I still want to teach because – when both parties are receptive – teaching is healing. But I'd also like to have my own company, as my father did in his fifties and sixties. I'd like to include amateurs and professionals, young people, old people, and I'd like to choreograph pieces that encompass people's experiences in life and reflect the meaning of it all…I just hope that somebody – God, the universe, the angels – is listening and will give me the male energy I need to carry it through!

APRIL '07

Photograph: Tribe of Doris, 2003

Ayodele Scott

SIERRA LEONE

Drumming is the source of life, it's spirit, it's pulse, it's feeling, it's enjoyment. It's something that's so essential, it's quintessential, to existence. I beat on things all the time – I beat on the steering wheel, I beat on the table, I beat on pots and pans in my kitchen – my fingers are never still. I'm constantly thinking in rhythms. But drumming is also a craft you can learn – it's a very good craft that takes you places nothing else – maybe singing – can take you so quickly. I love to sing. Singing is like – you *have* to sing. How can you talk and not sing?

Bands come and go. Whenever I have a new idea I have a new band, they grow, they die. I play with Baka Beyond, that's African rhythm, Celtic melody – but at the moment I have so many things… I'm going on this pilgrimage. I don't like the sea, it's not my thing, but then this opportunity arose and I have to follow the call.

Sameboat project is a ritual redemptive retracing of the Atlantic Slave Triangle. Many people, my people, other people's people, perished in that place we call the Middle Passage, and they are still there, waiting. We have to lay the spirits of the ancestors to rest and we have to neutralise the negativity of that place they call the Middle Passage.

Black people, white people. It's not about hatred and exclusion and all that stuff. It's about dealing with it. We both participated in the trade, yes, black people sold black people to white people. In those times we were strangers, you had your assumptions, we had ours. We said you were bad, you said we were idiots. OK, that's that. Now I have children who are mixed heritage – they know about and have been to Africa, but they live in England. We have to make things positive for them in the future, so they don't have this feeling of subjection, of oppression. This 2007, this Abolition 200, it's about finding a way of saying, 'OK can we think about those times?' It's about redeeming the spirit of our shared history.

We start with a performance in Bristol called Mami Wata and the Black Atlantic – Mami Wata is the Mother Goddess of the Sea and the Black Atlantic is the Middle Passage that we rename the Black Atlantic. There'll be costumes and drama and music and dance and we'll have a cast of about forty people – local people, children – and we'll work out a story about those times, with imagery and symbolism and ideology and emotions – because it's our shared heritage and if we can creatively find a way of playing with that, we'll feel at peace with ourselves in this here and now, in this twenty-first century, in this modern liberal world.

From Bristol we go to France, Spain, Portugal – we do performances there – then Cape Verde, Senegal, Gambia, Guinea Bissau, Guinea itself, and from Guinea we go to Freetown, Sierra Leone, my hometown. We do the Christmas thing there, and some time after that, we cross the Atlantic and from Africa to Trinidad we lay a line of red cotton like a line of blood or an umbilical cord and we'll do this ritual symbolic cleansing of the Middle Passage, with music and song and a thousand prayers played in the open air. And from Trinidad we go to Tobago, Jamaica, then home.

Growing up in Freetown was heaven. There were so many things happening in terms of music, in terms of theatre, in terms of just living. It's alive, it's vibrant, it's – and all I had to do was live it, there was no awareness I was learning – it was the best grounding a child could have. So that is something I cherish. The Freetown I grew up in was vibrating with expression, music, dance, theatre, food, smell, character, movement, colour.

I came over here when I was 26. Several years later the war started. It went on for nine, ten years and it was gruesome, absolutely gruesome, grotesque. Friends and family? I don't even know where some of them are. Dogs became not frightened of human beings, vultures became, I don't know, emptying the town. But now people want, they want to come back – because the children, the children who were growing up during that time – they've never played, and psychologically when you grow into an adult and you've never played there's a gap in your life. So in Freetown there's a mental and emotional drain, because some people haven't played, they've never been cuddled, and all they know is guns and drugs.

So that's the other reason why I'm doing this thing. I brought with me from Africa the music, the dance, the theatre and I came to this place where I mixed it with training and thinking. So now I want to take something back – because there are still people who knew me when I was little, they made it through the war, they're still alive, I've got my cousin, I've got a few other guys, they're not dead and then we'll all get together and we'll jump skin to skin because in Freetown I can do that because from the bottom of the street to the top of the street they'll be saying 'Ayo's doing this', and the old people will say, 'Ayo? Is he back?'

APRIL '07

Photograph: African Heartbeat, Bristol Zoological Gardens, 2003

Chartwell Dutiro

ZIMBABWE

When I was a baby my mother used to put me on her back when she went to *bira* ceremonies to sing for the ancestors. All through the night I must have listened to the sound of mbira and my mother's voice singing. I grew up with mbira all around me, sometimes kicking them sometimes sitting on them. It was my brother, Chikomborero, and one or two other people in the village who taught me to play.

When I was a bit older, I started to play for the spirit medium at ritual ceremonies where mbira is played to summon the spirits of the ancestors to possess the medium so people can ask for guidance and healing. If you go to my village today it's like an African hospital – people go there to be healed from Harare and from as far away as England.

In those days Zimbabwe was Rhodesia. It was a colonised country with an apartheid system. To the British, and especially to the missionaries who had come to teach us about Jesus and the bible, mbira music was the music of the devil. In 1896 and 1897 a female spirit medium, Mbuya NeHanda, who was committed to upholding Shona culture, helped to organise the resistance to colonial rule that was part of the First War of Independence. This

powerful woman was eventually captured, tried and sentenced to death. After that *bira* ceremonies were seen as political gatherings and both they and the music were banned.

My mother was always very special to me. I think she recognised that I wasn't an ordinary child – that I'd probably been chosen by the ancestors to play this instrument. Sometimes people would ask me to play when I had blisters and my fingers were thumping with pain and my mother would say, 'You have to remember that you are playing the music of your ancestors – the strength does not end.' And I began to understand that when people came from Harare where they worked for colonialists and they felt that their spirits had been suffocated, they needed to come back to the village and listen to the sound of mbira.

I came to England on a project called Strong Winds and Soft Earth Landings. It was a multimedia project using mbira players and jazz musicians to look at the relationship between Zimbabwe and Britain. While I was doing that I met Lucy Duran, who works at the University of London, and she encouraged me to do a degree in ethnomusicology. At first I associated ethnomusicology with people like Bruno Nettle who wrote about African music as 'primitive music' or 'the music of an uncivilised people' – and I wasn't interested. But then I realised that there is no definition of ethnomusicology – it is what you make of it, and I liked the idea of looking at other cultures through the eyes of music. So I decided to do it and then this book came out of it – *Zimbabwean Mbira Music on an International Stage* – and people can look at that and say, 'Yes. Here is an African man, a Zimbabwean musician talking about what he does with his instrument…'

I also have my own band, Spirit Talk Mbira. We have guitars – lead, rhythm and bass – drum kit, saxophone, trombone, trumpet and mbira, and the musicians are from many different cultures. In the past people have refused to book me at festivals because they want to put me into a box where I only play with African musicians – but one of my strongest beliefs is that music can build bridges between cultures and that's the only time we cross that stereotype of them and us.

I work with other musicians as well. At the moment I'm collaborating with a string quartet in Dawlish, and in 2005 I was commissioned by the Royal Shakespeare Company to compose and perform a mbira piece for 'Breakfast with Mugabe'. But it's strange that whatever I compose, arrange or play on mbira is influenced by the culture of my childhood. I will never compose a song that sounds like a pop song because mbira for me is spiritual music, imbued with the voices of my ancestors.

I love playing and I love composing, but my most important work is probably teaching. I teach mbira and Shona songs and I work with Tribe of Doris, the University of Plymouth, an agency called Devon Arts in Schools Initiative… and what is fascinating for me is how the sound – I could call this the voices of the ancestors – how it touches different people from different cultures in the same way as the music touches Shona people. I have played mbira here in England and people cry and have visions because they are touching the ancestors – their ancestors, my ancestors – through the music of mbira.

Looking back I know that my mother was right – that it's a calling for me to be here. I didn't choose to come to England and I didn't choose to make a life out of mbira but the ancestors paved my way and this is where I was led. Sometimes I feel that I'm a cultural vicar, in a strange sort of way I'm a missionary – but not in an evangelical sense – I'm just guiding people to understand their ancestry and their spirituality.

JULY '07

Photograph: Tribe of Doris, 2007

Mbira are made out of hand-forged metal keys attached to a wooden board. At the bottom of the board is a metal plate with conch shells or bottle tops that bounce around and vibrate. Sometimes the whole thing is placed inside a gourd called a deze *which makes the sound resonate. To play mbira you use both thumbs and sometimes, depending on the number of keys, one of your forefingers. The wood is called* mubva maropa, *'the wood that bleeds', because when you cut into it it oozes red sap. People listen to the wood before they make mbira to make sure that it has a good sound and the blacksmiths who forge the keys bless them and tune them to the voices of their ancestors.*

Alejandro Velasco

SPAIN

My mother and my aunt were both flamenco dancers – they danced with different companies all over the world – and my father was a flamenco manager. So I and all of my sisters – I have eight sisters – have been surrounded by flamenco since we were born. All of us danced when we were younger, but I'm the only one who has gone on to dance professionally and to teach flamenco.

I was seven when I started to train at the Conservatory in Madrid. At the beginning it was like a fairytale. I went there with a group of friends – all of us with our dresses and pink tights and our hair done specially. We went for about two hours every day, after school. We didn't just do flamenco, we also did contemporary dance, classical ballet and *escuela bolera*.

Growing up with flamenco was great, but there was also responsibility. My family was very discerning and I often felt that I'd never be good enough. My mother used to tell me that I was a really good dancer and I remember saying, 'Oh, Mum, I'm not so sure'. But she always believed in me. Always gave me support.

I left the Conservatory when I was twelve – although every year I went back for the exams – and started to dance with a private

teacher. This teacher, Maria del Carmen Romero – who I thank from the bottom of my heart – was like a second mother to me. She was wise and encouraging, but she was also strict. Sometimes – when she seemed to correct every detail – I thought she was *too* strict. But looking back I can see that she *had* to be strict, that her endless corrections have made me the dancer I am. To an outsider flamenco can look like a wild and spontaneous dance, but there's so much to learn and *everything* counts – the alignment of the whole body, the hands, the shoulders, the hips. You have to move everything and you have to move everything right – because if you move the shoulders and then you move the hips the wrong way, you're going to look really strange.

But flamenco isn't just about technique. You have to be able to communicate with people; you have to have something spicy. That's what makes flamenco such a passionate dance. I love technique – but I also love to play with the audience. For example, there are different types of dance: there's *sole*, which means solitary, not necessarily sad, but introspective, and there's *bulería*, which is faster and has more of a party mood. I love to start off slowly, so the audience thinks I'm going to be quiet and serious and then suddenly I'll pick up speed and start smiling...

I came over here three and a half years ago. I thought it would be difficult to find work teaching and performing, but people are really interested. At the moment I'm teaching six group classes and several private students. I also perform regularly at venues throughout England and Wales. Sometimes I think people see me performing and say, 'Ooh, I'd love to be able to do that'. Most of my students are women – and I think that's because of the way you can express yourself in flamenco. It's a strong dance – you can do soft things but it's still a strong dance. Sometimes people say that a woman who dances flamenco strongly can be quite bossy!

British people learn flamenco just like Spanish ones. If you're passionate about it and come to all the classes, there's no difference. Maybe Spanish people learn the rhythm and the clapping more quickly because they've grown up with the music. But I can't say that every Spanish person is good at flamenco. Perhaps the most difficult thing for British people is to separate the hips from the shoulders and not to dance with a straight torso. But all of my students work hard, and I'm really impressed with their progress.

For the moment, I'm happy living in Bristol. Sometimes Spanish people come to my classes and performances and say, 'This is fantastic, I feel as though I'm in Spain again!' So I create my own little patch of Spain around me. I'd like to go to Japan as well – the Japanese love flamenco. But in the end I want to live in Spain. My family is there and we're very close – I love my nieces and nephews as though they were my own children – and I can't imagine settling anywhere else.

MAY '07

Photograph: Bristol Harbour Festival, 2005

Alphonse Daudet Touna

CAMEROON

I'm mainly a percussionist, an African percussionist, but I'm influenced by percussion from all over the world. My favourite instrument, the one I relate to most is the balafon, which is a kind of Cameroonian xylophone that goes right back to the times of our ancestors. Even today when there's a wedding or – for some tribes – a funeral, or any kind of celebration or community event, we play the balafon. It's an instrument that's both percussive and melodic so you can play it with drums, on its own or as an accompaniment to singing.

These balafons I made myself, here in my workshop. The wood and the gourds I order from Cameroon. It's a special kind of wood, called *meia* – which we use for making boats because it's resistant to humidity and lasts for years – and the clarity of sound it produces is really amazing. The gourds were originally used for grain storage or as bottles for palm wine or oil. They're brittle – like glass. People often ask how I learned to make balafons, and it's difficult because I don't really know. In Africa we learn by eye and by ear, so I suppose I watched and listened to what people were doing around me. And then when I trained as an engineer it opened my eyes to design and I began to expand on the traditional method. At one time balafons were small, with only

one or one and a half octaves but now I make some that are two, three or even four octaves, and also some that are chromatic so you can play them more easily with other musical instruments.

My band is called Hélélé and the music we play is Cameroonian rhythm mixed with Western musical instruments to create a kind of musical colour we call Afro-Jazz. The other musicians are mostly from England, and each time we practise it's like a little school – I learn about theory and how to write music and they learn about African rhythm and polyrhythm, which isn't always easy for English people. I sing in my own language but sometimes I mix it with French and English and other Cameroonian languages – we have nearly two hundred languages in Cameroon – and the message behind it is what's happening in the world – now, in the past and in the future. There's so much injustice in the world…

African drumming is very popular at the moment – in Europe and America and all over the world – and we should look into why that is. To me rhythm is part of being alive, our bodies need it. It's also a kind of meditation – you can meditate through being quiet or you can meditate through rhythm. If you're very quiet and you listen to yourself, you can hear a rhythm and if you focus on that and work on it you can learn to develop it. African drumming also brings people together. I work with adults and children from different cultures, and after five minutes' drumming they speak the same language, they smile at each other, without constantly having to ask, 'What's your name?' That's very special to me.

I also teach – but that word makes me laugh. Everyone in the world is learning. Life is *about* learning, and if I have a particular skill I'll do my best to give others the opportunity to benefit from it. Learning and teaching are two sides of the same coin and just as I'll never stop learning, so I'll never stop teaching. But yes, I'm a qualified teacher in Cameroon and in England. I teach adults and I teach in schools. Last month I ran a drumming workshop at the Commonwealth Museum to introduce children to African Culture and to talk about the slave trade. That was so popular. I also work with drug and alcohol abusers, and I play balafon to people in care homes. Once when I was teaching special needs children this little girl came up to me – she came up in her wheelchair and she hugged me and stroked my hair and said, 'Uhhh Uhhhhhh'. For me giving a little happiness to someone like her makes everything worthwhile.

But at the moment I'm a bit unstable. I can't plan anything because I don't know what's going to happen tomorrow. One day they just sent me the news, 'Oh, you don't fit the immigration rules, you're doing more and more teaching and you're supposed to be a musician'. But I've been in this country for five years – and nothing's changed – I'm doing what I've always been doing, and they've renewed my work permit twice.

Really they should warn you, talk to each person individually and give you a chance to defend yourself – not just tick a box on the computer and say, 'OK, stand up, go now!' We're human! If I go now how many things will be wasted? I'm teaching in four different schools – how many children will suffer, how many people who come here for drumming and balafon classes, how many musicians? In my little band we have plans together. I'm not saying that I'm anything special… but in this world everyone needs a mission and for me being here doing the work that I'm doing – this is my mission.

MARCH '07

Photograph: Bristol Refugee Week, 2004

In February 2007 the Home Office declined to renew Alphonse's work permit and, despite a vociferous local campaign, at the time of publication he remains under threat of deportation.

Zdzisława (SYLVIA) Żukowska

POLAND/ITALY

My mother came from Wołyń in eastern Poland. One night soon after the Russians invaded Poland, a group of soldiers knocked on her parents' door and told them to pack their bags. They gave them half an hour to gather their things and then took them to the station, loaded them onto cattle trucks and deported them to Siberia. My grandmother died soon afterwards, my grandfather was sent to work in the salt-mines, and my mother – who was fifteen – chopped wood in the forest in order to provide for her younger brothers and sister. My father was also in Siberia at the time – wrongly accused of spying and sentenced to 25 years' hard labour. But it wasn't until much later that my parents met.

After Germany invaded Russia – and Russia joined the allies – an amnesty was declared for all Poles in Soviet prisoner-of-war camps. These civilians – including my father – were taken to the south of Russia where they were trained to be soldiers in the newly formed Polish Army, which later joined the Allied Forces. During the war they travelled – with all the children who had become orphans in Siberia – from Russia, to Iran, Iraq, India, Africa, Palestine and eventually Italy. It was here that my parents met, and I was born.

I don't know why they came to England after the war – I suppose because they were in the British forces and my father knew a bit of the language. We went from one displaced persons' camp to another. The camps were ex-forces, so after the army or the air force moved out, we took over the barracks. There was a big camp in Keevil, and when the camps were eventually closed, around 1957, all the Poles from Keevil moved to the nearest town, which was here – Trowbridge.

Our dance group Kujawy was started in 1960 – my husband was one of the founders. They hired a Polish choreographer from London who came and taught them the dances and brought some costumes, which our dressmaker was able to copy. They danced at weddings and parties and also at folk festivals – there were a lot more of them in those days – in Letterkenny, Dublin, Sidmouth, Chippenham…

I joined soon after I married in 1966. I had to learn the dances – there are a lot of different traditional dances from different areas but the main ones we do are Kujawiak, polka, oberek and Krakowiak. I was familiar with the music and the rhythm of course and I'd learned a few steps in Polish School and the Polish Scouting Movement. But the dancing is in you – the minute you hear the music, you're off, you're moving!

We rehearse twice a week – here in the Polish Club. And once a week we girls get together in the bar to work on our costumes. We have several costumes: the Krakowski is a dressy one that they used to wear in the king's court and it was also a wedding outfit. But there are peasant ones as well. Some of our costumes are forty years old and they're falling apart, so every Thursday we get together and sew. We've made our own blouses and skirts and aprons and we're now on the little jackets which take a long time, with all the beads and embroidery. The boys' jackets are too complicated for us, so we order those from Poland.

We try to keep all our Polish traditions alive. Most of the socials here at the Club have a Polish theme – we make Polish food and drink Polish vodka and beer. And most of us have a Polish Christmas with a big meal – twelve courses – on Christmas Eve. It takes weeks to prepare. We used to have to get some of the ingredients from Poland but now with this new generation of immigrants there are Polish delicatessens springing up all over the place. So if we like, we can even buy our *pirogi* here in Trowbridge, ready made!

When my children were little they loved to dance – and they loved to see their parents dance. I think they were very proud of us. We try to bring our children up bilingually, but it's difficult because English is obviously their first language. They all go to Polish School and the Polish Scouting Movement and most of them do a bit of Polish dancing – it's one of their proficiency badges in the scouts – and they also do performances with school. But Trowbridge is a small place for career-minded people. A lot of young people move away to colleges and jobs. My son is in the air force now and my daughter has her own family.

A lot of people who come from Poland say we're bigger Poles than they are in Poland – we're greater patriots. Not many people in Poland do the traditional dances any more – unless of course they're in a team or something. It's just like English people here with English traditional dancing – when it's on your doorstep you're not interested. But because we've never lived in Poland we're hungry for it, we need it, we want it. We're trying to get a choreographer over at the moment to teach us some more dances. We love the music, we love the rhythm and although we're all getting on a bit now and maybe some of the younger generation look at us and say, '*God*, dancing at *that* age!', we're young at heart and we really love it.

MAY '07
*Interviewed with the kind help of Roman Brzezicki
and members of Kujawy dance company*
*Photograph: (with Fred Potem)
Bristol Refugee Week, 2007*

Claudia Aurora
PORTUGAL

I have always felt a spiritual connection with Brazilian music and dance. I never knew where this came from because my parents – although they loved music – leaned towards England and America. But one day my great aunt drew up a family tree and discovered that my great great grandparents on my mother's side came to Spain, then Portugal, from Brazil.

I left school when I was really young. I knew then that I wanted to be a singer and dancer and that school was a waste of time. So I started to work in a factory and spent most of my earnings on books and CDs. I wanted to get right to the heart of Brazilian music, to learn about major artists like Elis Regina, Chico Buaraque and Vinicius de Morais. I scoured the shops for CDs and I listened to them over and over – I ate them. It was through bossa nova that I discovered my voice skills.

Dancing came later, when I was 21. I wanted to learn samba because I love the music but there was no teacher in the small town where I grew up. So one year I videoed the Rio Carnival, which is shown live on Portuguese television, and I spent hours, months – if not years – practising the samba in front of my mother's living room mirror.

My parents never really supported me in my career. My father would have liked me to work in an office and my mother wanted me to get married and have children. I felt that I was being limited by my family values and that to pursue my dream I needed to escape.

So I came to England to pick daffodils. I was with a group of friends and we travelled from Cornwall to Scotland, moving with the season. It was so cold. It was the hardest work I have ever done. But I was able to save a bit of money and with that I went back to Portugal, rented a flat and enrolled in a music school. I just went for an audition as a singer and they accepted me. It was classical singing, opera – to develop my voice and breathing skills. That was one year, intensive.

Afterwards I came back to England and settled in Cornwall. In the daytime I worked in a gallery and in the evenings I sang bossa nova. Then one year I was asked to go to Tribe of Doris to sing and teach samba. That was my gateway to Bristol and new opportunity… after that so many girls used to chase me for samba classes, and I kept saying no, I don't want to teach, but they just came to my house – first one, then two, three, five…

So I decided to go to Brazil and train. I first went to the dance school in Rio de Janeiro and then I went to Salvador da Bahia in the north, where I studied samba Baiano and samba reggae. Bahia is where the Portuguese brought African slaves 500 years ago, and samba Baiano is more earthy and grounded and closer to its African roots than the Carnival samba I'd learned in Portugal, which is more showgirl – more glitter and feathers. Samba reggae is a fusion of samba Baiano and reggae. It's a dance of the black people, a dance of the streets. Everyone does it – old people, children – the movements are beautiful and easy to learn and the music is so contagious that everyone just pours into the streets to enjoy themselves.

But then – when I was back in England – a strange thing happened. I went out and bought a fado CD. Fado is the traditional music of Portugal but because I've always felt this connection with Brazil, I'd never really listened to it. So I played the CD and I thought, 'This is amazing'. Sometimes as a joke I'd sing it to friends, and they'd say, 'You've got a really good fado voice,' and I'd go, 'Oh come on, I've never sung fado in my life – I don't even like it.' But the more I listened the more I fell in love with it. It's very passionate singing, very strong. You have to have a really strong voice to sing fado. It started in the eighteenth century in poor areas of Lisbon and it used to be sung by bohemians in dark, smoke-filled bars. It's all about longing – love, loss and the tragedy of human hearts.

Now I often sing fado in Bristol. The venues are usually packed and the feedback is great. But I need to decide what I really want to do, because at the moment I like far too many things. I think I'll settle for fado and carry on teaching samba reggae and samba Baiano because they keep me going and they help with my voice. Fado is in my culture, it's in my blood and when I sing it I feel intensely at home. But I only discovered it one year ago. I need to work on it as hard as I've worked on Brazilian music – I need to give it patience and I need to give it time.

AUGUST '07

Photograph: Ashton Court Festival, 2007

Sonal Barot
INDIA/UK

My grandparents migrated from Gujarat to East Africa in search of a better life for themselves and their children, and my parents were amongst the generation of Indians who were expelled from Uganda by Idi Amin. When I was a child growing up in Bristol my mother was determined to give me access to parts of my Indian heritage which she didn't have in East Africa. So when I was five or six I started to learn Mohiniyattam, which is one of the seven styles of Indian classical dance and several years later I started Bharata Natyam, which is the style I practise now.

At first it was a weekly battle to get me to classes. Indian classical dance is built on grace and elegance and I often felt awkward learning the steps and performing the movements. But when I was thirteen something suddenly clicked and I fell in love with it.

Bharata Natyam has its roots in Hinduism. Many of the temples used to have their own dancers, *devadasis*, and there are stone carvings of dancers in a lot of the ancient temples. But in the early twentieth century, during the time of British rule, people started to associate temple dancing with sexual exploitation and prostitution, and the tradition became less popular. Then in the 1930s some pioneering artists started to systemise and categorise

the steps, creating what's now called Bharata Natyam. No one knows exactly how closely Bharata Natyam resembles the ancient tradition depicted in stone.

The dance has two main features – the first focuses on steps and geometry and the second, *abhinaya*, tells a story. *Abhinaya* usually expresses devotion to God and is told with the help of facial expressions and hand gestures called *mudras*. The costumes are made of silk saris, which you take to a special Bharata Natyam tailor who adapts them. You can have up to three fans going up the front or you can have a single fan at the side. I think you can probably also buy them ready-made now – but that takes all the fun out of getting measured up and choosing your own design!

Most of my training I've done with India Dance Wales, either in Cardiff or in Bristol. My teacher, Kiran Ratna who started the school, was born in Punjab, came to Cardiff to do her undergraduate studies, and then stayed on. At times when I was training so hard that I had to take time off school in Bristol, she would put me up in her home and look after me. And it was she who organised my *Arangetram,* which is the first public solo performance you do when your teacher feels you are ready.

When I left school I decided to go to Chennai and see Bharata Natyam in its home setting. It was incredible. Dance is everywhere – it's in people's body language, it's in their postures, it's in the gestures they use to express themselves. I've seen people in their seventies dancing for hours, partly because they have none of the problems that we have here like stiffness and injury from cold weather and badly heated studios and having to struggle to fit it in because it's not part of your culture. Dance is just there, it's part of life.

At the moment I'm trying to figure out where my career is going. I have a degree in history and I hope to work as a human rights advocate. I suppose if I really wanted to I could make a career out of dancing, but it wouldn't be easy. I'll always dance – but for my own enjoyment. There are times in which to push and times in which to hold back…

Part of the reason I love teaching is that it helps me to practise. I teach mainly in schools, as an introduction to Hinduism, and I teach a weekly class in Bristol. Most of my students are of Indian heritage but anyone can learn. One of the best Bharata Natyam dancers I know, Megan Lloyd, is Welsh. She didn't start learning until she was in her early twenties and she now teaches and performs for India Dance Wales. The power of the mind is always greater than the power of the body and if the mind says, 'I want to do this', it will happen.

Learning Bharata Natyam has taught me so much more about my heritage than dance. It has taught me about religion and mythology, music, and the Indian attitude to learning which is all about deference and humility. It has also taught me to use my body to train my mind. Bharata Natyam is like yoga in that it aims through posture, alignment and breathing, to reach a point where your mind is still. Looking back as an adult I feel so grateful to my mother for taking me to classes, and I hope that if ever I have children they too will want to learn.

OCTOBER '07

Photograph: Bristol Harbour Festival, 2007

Euridice Oyaga de Hollis

COLOMBIA

The candles in the photograph are a present. The men give them to the ladies to say, 'Please dance with me'. In Colombia we do this dance at night in the open air and the candles are lit. It looks so beautiful. If you're a good dancer you're offered as many candles as you can hold… I remember when I was about seven a boy came up to me with one candle and I said, 'Sorry, I can't dance for that!' So he went all the way to the shop to buy me some more.

Music and dancing have always been part of my life. My mother is a well-known *cantadora*, Totó de Momposina, my grandmother was a *cantadora* and dancer and my grandfather was a drummer. When I was six my grandmother started a dance company and for a while I performed with my brothers and sisters and cousins. Most of our dances came from the Caribbean coastal area of Colombia, where my parents and grandparents used to live before they moved to Bogotá. Caribbean music is really interesting. You can see the influence of all the people who've ever lived in that area – the indigenous Indians, the Spanish colonisers and the African slaves who were initially brought to Colombia to work in the mines and plantations. In some of the African dances you can tell from the way the dancers move that at one time they must have been wearing chains.

I was very happy as a child. I remember going to my mother's concerts and sitting on the edge of the stage singing along because I knew all her songs and when she was researching traditional music I travelled with her to the Caribbean coast, to the Andes, to the Chanis Orientalis in the east of Colombia. But when I was nine my parents separated. I didn't see much of my mother after that – she was often touring in Europe and then she went to live in Paris for five years. My grandmother's company had folded by then but I joined a dance company at school and I studied traditional dance and a bit of ballet with different teachers in different schools.

And then when I was 18 my mother came back to Bogotá. I'd left school by then so I started to perform with her again and in 1991 when she toured Europe, my brother and sister and I went with her. It was on that trip that I met my husband, John, who is my mother's manager. After the tour John came back to Colombia to work with my mother and on our next trip to Europe, two years later, he and I visited his parents in England. We've been here ever since.

At first I found it hard living in England. I'd been used to having my family around me. My grandmother had a big house in Bogotá where I grew up with some of my uncles and aunts and cousins, and the rest of the family lived nearby. So when I came to England I felt very isolated.

But I started to teach in schools. I used to do one day a week teaching the dances I learned as a child, and in conjunction with this the kids also learned percussion, history, craft and cooking. At the end of the course we brought all these subjects together in a Colombian performance. The children loved it. I also teach at Tribe of Doris, where my mother and brother both taught before me.

One year at Tribe of Doris we met some other Colombian musicians and we decided to form a company, Colores de mi Tierra. John and I have five children and the three eldest perform with us – Maria and Oriana sing and dance and Paolo plays *bombo*. John is our manager. We don't get a chance to meet very often to practise be-cause we all live in different places, but we're planning a lot more concerts and at half term we're recording in the studio.

I don't know if our children will perform when they're older, but at least I know that they have the basis, and if they want to take it further, they can. As a family we're very involved with music. John manages and produces bands from different parts of the world and we all go to festivals so the children are exposed to other types of music, not just Colombian. It's important to me not only that we keep our own tradition alive but that we work with other musicians and dancers to make it richer. I didn't realise until I came here that musically we have so much in common with different parts of the world.

So I teach and I perform, but most of the time I'm a housewife and mother. Maybe I'm old fashioned but I think that if you have kids you have the responsibility to provide a proper root for them to be something when they grow up. A lot of people are so busy making money that family no longer really exists. And when family no longer exists traditions like music die out. But singing and dancing aren't just things people do, they're part of our nature – and when as a culture we lose them it's like losing a limb.

OCTOBER '07

Photograph: Tribe of Doris, 2007

Dr Joel
INDIA

My parents noticed that at the age of three I was able to pick out tunes by ear on my toy piano. Soon after that they arranged for me to have music lessons in Mumbai where we lived. It was the kind of musical education in which I was taught musical notation and composition. I had an amazing teacher and by the time I was six, writing music came as naturally to me as writing with letters and words. It's a gift that has stayed with me all through my life.

My grandfather was a conductor and orchestra leader in the court of a maharaja. My parents also loved music, both Western and Indian, but my father was determined that for me, unlike my grandfather, music should be a hobby, not a career.

I trained to be a doctor near Madras – now called Chennai – which is the capital of south Indian or Carnatic music, and although I took my studies seriously, I made it a project to immerse myself in the musical glories of Chennai. I found a guru, Sri T.R. Harihara Sharma, who many people think is the greatest ever teacher of Carnatic rhythm. He used to sit cross-legged on a huge wooden swing suspended from the ceiling by chains, and while I squatted at his feet learning my rhythms, he would swing gently backwards and forwards.

In Carnatic music every instrument imitates the voice, so you learn a vocal language before you learn an instrument. For rhythm this language is *konnakol*, for melody it's *sargam*. *Konnakol* can be performed as a vocal art in its own right, or it can be articulated through a musical instrument. Once you've learnt *konnakol* it's relatively easy to adapt it to any instrument. It takes only a short while for example to absorb the basic features of the *mridangam*, which is the ancient two-sided drum, the *ghatam* which is a clay pot, or the *kanjira* which is the south Indian tambourine.

My medical career took me to Geneva, to the World Health Organisation, where I helped devise and put into practice a tuberculosis control strategy which is now used worldwide. It was a job I loved but it left me no time for anything else. Without music in my life, I started to feel that part of me had been amputated.

So I left my job and came to England, which is where my wife is from. Now I could say I'm almost a full-time musician: I compose, I perform and I teach.

Dr Joel is my stage name. I perform with traditional Indian musicians at festivals and concert halls throughout the world and I perform my own music, which is a blend of Carnatic and Western traditions. Sometimes for my original work I'm accompanied by a *veena,* which is one of the oldest south Indian instruments, but generally I'm solo with a keyboard, a *tanpura*, ankle bells and my voice for *konnakol* and lyrics. I use my special keyboard because it allows me to glide between notes in the way that we Indian musicians do. The *tanpura*, which I use sampled or prerecorded, provides the drone that you hear in the background of all Indian music; the ankle bells mark the rhythm; and the lyrics – well I love poetry, I love writing songs and it's a way to present this rich and ancient tradition in a way that everyone can enjoy.

Teaching is very important to me. Sometimes I see myself as a kind of missionary for this art form that I love, *konnakol*. Classes of primary-school children are possibly my favourites, because we have a lot of fun singing 'Ravenous like a tiger' and some of my other songs, and within a couple of hours they astonish their teachers with how much they can do. I also teach recording artists – singers, such as Sheila Chandra, guitarists, drummers, saxophonists – anyone who wants to enrich their rhythmic practice. *Konnakol* is a universal language – it can help anyone compose, perform, or appreciate the rhythm of any music in the world – and in my view it should be part of the general musical education everywhere. It seems a crime to confine these treasures to one tradition – it's like saying that Shakespeare should be read by only English people...

No, it wasn't a particularly easy decision to leave the World Health Organisation and my medical career. But am I happy with it? Am I happy to be breathing?

NOVEMBER '07

Photograph: Tribe of Doris, 2007

Penny Avery

JAMAICA/UK

I was born in Chichester. My natural parents are from Jamaica but – apart from my mother's name which I found out from Social Services – I know nothing about them. My adoptive parents are white. I have one white brother but he's eight years older than me, so a lot of the time it was just me, my mum and my dad. It wasn't always easy being the only black kid in a white family and white primary school, but overall it was a great upbringing – I couldn't have asked for more.

I was never really bullied at school. Sometimes I'd get called things like 'monkey face' – which wasn't very nice – but kids can be nasty and silly and when you're at school you're going to get it for one reason or another. If I look at it from a positive point of view I could say that growing up in a white environment gave me confidence in certain situations, but the downside was that I grew up shy of my own people. I remember when I was very young there was one Jamaican family near us and I just stared at them, completely in awe.

I met my first husband Bozie on a train station in Swansea when I was seventeen. Bozie is from Ghana – he's a drummer and dancer – and it was he who introduced me to African culture. He took me

to my first festival where I did a workshop in African dance and I just thought, 'Wow!' And since that day I've kept on dancing. It was all west African dance, which I learned from different teachers in Bristol, where we lived, and at festivals. After a while a friend of mine called Ben asked me to choreograph three dance pieces for his band Drum Orchestra, and when they got a grant from the National Lottery to go on tour, I joined them as a dancer. We performed at arts theatres and festivals and taught in schools all over the country.

After I left Drum Orchestra I went to Senegal to train. I stayed with the family of a friend of mine, Migatte, and they were a family of performers so they were constantly dancing and drumming. I went there twice, and both times there was some kind of celebration going on so in the night time they'd get out the drums and we'd dance and dance. And in the daytime the kids taught me new dances in the compound. It was a fantastic way to learn and I loved being part of an African family.

When I came back to England it occurred to me that I was doing all this dancing but I'd never been formally trained. I'd always been very sporty at school and my parents had encouraged me in that, but the only dancing I did was in my bedroom behind closed doors. So I enrolled for a HND in contemporary dance. It was a fantastic course – very creative, very expressive – and it gave me the confidence to say, 'Yes, I'm a professional dancer.'

My dancing took a different direction after that. I started to work with Denise Rowe, who was on the course with me and has the same Jamaican heritage. We're both strong dancers but in different ways and when we dance duets, it really seems to work. So we formed a company, Tolo ko Tolo, which means Life is Life in the language of the Baka, in Cameroon. I suppose our dancing is African Fusion or African Contemporary.

Like all dancers I sometimes worry about the future and what will happen when I'm too old to dance. So I decided to do a degree in dance which I hoped would lead to a teaching job and the security of a salary. At first I was doing it full time, travelling to Cardiff four days a week. But the course is quite academic with lots of essays to write and I missed dancing so much that I switched over to part time. It means that I won't finish for another four or five years but at least I'll be dancing while I'm still young.

So now I teach African dance and hip hop, I choreograph and perform with Denise, I work three days a week in a factory and I'm a single mother with two kids – who at the end of the day come first. I almost earn a living from dancing but I've always been a bit slack on the business front. Now I'm determined. What I'd really like is to get funding so Denise and I can spend time in the studio, creating, choreographing, bringing in other dancers, performing at theatres and festivals and doing workshops in schools.

That's my long term plan – but in the short term I'm going to Jamaica on holiday, and I'm *so* excited! I'm going with my two kids and it's the first time for all of us. I've never been able to afford it before but a friend of a friend says we can stay in her villa in Runaway Bay and she's able to get us cheap flights. I think there's a dance school there so I'm hoping to learn some Jamaican dances. And I really want to – I'd love to – track down my mum and my dad and any relatives I've got out there. I mean, I don't think I've been traumatised by my past – it all makes you stronger – but when I was growing up it did make me sad and it still makes me sad. Maybe it won't be feasible this time, but you never know, a friend of mine went out there expecting nothing and the next thing he knew he bumped into his dad.

It's strange, I've always loved Africa and felt drawn to Africa more than Jamaica – but now that I'm going to Jamaica, I've got this strange feeling here in my heart…

NOVEMBER '07
Photograph: Tribe of Doris, 2003

Rachel
de Garang

SUDAN

I was born in Sudan but when I was six years old the war broke out and I left Sudan and moved between Kenya, Zambia, Ethiopia, Uganda and England. Although my father was in the Church he'd got involved in politics and one day he was arrested. So the family decided to break him out of prison – if they'd left him there he'd probably have been tortured or killed. We had to leave Sudan that night.

Not until I was about fourteen did dance appear in my life. I was sent to boarding school in Kenya. It was a girls' school and all the girls came from different tribes – in Kenya, in Uganda and in Tanzania – and I started to realise that people moved differently, there was different music, and they would sing in their own languages, and that really amazed me. I suppose when we danced around the dormitory and things we were doing a mixture of traditional and popular African dance – that is Highlife and Soukous.

My family was back in Sudan by then, and when I went home for the holidays my father made it a task to get us all dancing together in the evening. He was Minister for Culture at the time so everywhere he went he was entertained by different tribes. They would put on all these fantastic events and I'd sit there at the front

with my dad and I'd watch and listen and take it all in. I suppose I just absorbed the traditional dances.

When I was seventeen I got married – it was an arranged marriage – and I came to England with my husband. Unfortunately my husband didn't approve of my dance, so it took a back seat for over ten years. It was just me, him and the three kids. But thankfully he went away for a couple of years and I thought, 'OK I can stick my head outside the door again'. Soon afterwards I was offered a job with a community radio station in Bristol, so I left my husband and came here with the kids and suddenly there was all this opportunity. It was unbelievable and I thought, 'Right, this is where I'm supposed to be. This is it – Bristol'.

Every Thursday night I used to go to Club 49 on Christmas Steps, where a band called FNAAZ played Soukous, and one day they invited me to come and dance with them. It was fantastic. I felt suddenly that this door had opened and I was in there. I was in this world I hadn't known existed, and there were threads of my life and a very strong connection with the memory of my father and – this sounds strange – I lived the memory in the movement.

One night a student from Bristol University came to one of our FNAAZ gigs and said, 'Please, please come and do some dance classes'. I'd never taught formally, but when it comes to dance I don't do too much, 'Oh dear me, maybe I could, maybe I couldn't'. And the best thing was that they were going to pay me! What I really enjoy about teaching is the feeling when you show some-one something and they show it back to you and it looks good and better. And I love performing with my students – sharing that space, looking at each other and just grinning. We're having a little party on stage between the dancers and the musicians – it's much more exciting than dancing on my own.

My first step into the mainstream world of dance was when I started a degree in Dance at Bath Spa University and the words I'd use to describe it are culturally, physically and intellectually challenging. I felt as though my whole world of dance was being ripped apart and I didn't know if I'd ever be able to dance again. There was one girl of mixed heritage – from Bermuda I think – but everyone else was white. So the background of all the students and all the teachers was ballet – you know, held upper body, very precise; first, fifth, eighth position. This is what we were expected to do in the technique classes and I'd think, 'Mm beautiful, lovely, but *I* can't move like that'. There's a particular shape an African dance body has as opposed to a Western ballet-trained dancer and it wasn't until I found a book about this that I actually began to understand where I fit in.

That first year – which I did full time – practically killed me. I felt that I didn't belong, that no one wanted to work with me because my ideas weren't 'contemporary dance' and wouldn't be recognised by the tutors. But looking back this was a process I had to go through, and I'm so glad I didn't just say, 'Oh this isn't for me, I'm off!' I've learned such a lot from the course, and when I finish what I'd *really* like to do is find a job in a university or a big dance institution where I can work within the mainstream but introduce and promote African dance because in the future this would benefit not only African dancers like me but dancers and audiences from all over the world – because African dance has so much to offer us all.

FEBRUARY '07

Photograph: Bristol Harbour Festival, 2004

Samuel Hutchinson

JAMAICA

My father says that on the night I was conceived my parents had been to a Nat King Cole concert and the reason I'm a singer is that my conception was a musical thing with Nat King Cole watching over us. Sometimes I think of doing a Nat King Cole tribute, you know, getting smartly dressed and singing all those songs I love so well, 'Dance ballerina, dance, do a pirouette...'

My parents left Jamaica when I was a toddler; England needed labour at the time and invited thousands of West Indians to come over and work. So my brother and I were brought up by our grandparents. We had a beautiful childhood – my grandmother lived in Kingston at first but when our neighbourhood started to get violent she moved us all to the country. Overnight she built a grocery store and from the age of ten I was the manager. I remember going on the bus to take our orders of flour and sugar and basic necessities to the wholesalers in the local town and having to make sure I was back in time to help unload and check the order when the delivery arrived.

I was twelve when our parents sent for us. I remember my first day at St George's School in Bristol – I was really excited because I'd always done well at school and my ambition was to become a

lawyer. But when I'd been there for about a month the headmaster stood me up in front of the whole school and praised me in such a way that some of the white kids turned against me. They started to bully me, and to defend myself I started to fight.

My outlet was my parents' record collection. I used to love listening to voices like Ben E. King and Dickie Valentine and their melancholy songs, not quite gospel but with elements of gospel in them – because although I was young I was intrigued by all those things – love, longing, darkness – and maybe because of my upbringing in the Church it felt like the start of me expressing what was really inside me.

Gradually – I don't know if it was because of the bullying or because the work was getting too hard for me – I lost interest in school. I started to spend more time at the sports club, and of course there was music…

My younger brother Dennis who was born in England has always been a big influence on me. He used to play trombone in the school band, and from an early age our father bought him equipment so he could practise. Now he plays mainly keyboard but he's learned to incorporate other instruments through it, and he's a great programmer of drums. The two of us have always been very close – we've worked in so many bands together and when he started Jungle Red I was the singer.

Jungle Red is mainly a reggae band and although I have always enjoyed performing reggae, I see myself as more of a soul or jazz singer. I was very moved by some of Bob Marley's early work and like everyone else when I was growing up I listened to Desmond Decca and Jimmy Cliff, but for me reggae lacks a certain musical sophistication, and the singers I've listened to and wanted to emulate have been more the Sam Cooks of this world.

Over the years I've sung in so many bands I've lost count, but the main ones have been the Panthers (who later became Talisman), which was another reggae band, and the Tommy Hawkins Band, which had a regular slot at the Locarno in the centre of Bristol. We used to perform Come Dancing songs like 'Autumn Leaves' and 'Let me Love you Tonight'. And then I came third in a national competition at the Kings Country Club – singing to a seated audience of 4000 and broadcast on television – and I was briefly signed by Polydor, who said they wanted to make me the next Johnny Mathis.

So one way or another there's always been work – a tour coming up, a recording session, different bands wanting a singer – but recently I've had certain setbacks and problems with my health, so I haven't been working so much. Times have changed I think and instead of expecting opportunities to come to me as they always used to do, I'll have to go out and look for them.

One day I went to an evangelical church in Bristol, and because they knew I was a singer they asked me to perform. So I took one of their regular songs and improvised the lyrics in gospel style while the congregation sang the chorus. Since then they've invited me back many times and I've got into a position where I could easily write and record gospel music – because I find it really uplifting. But I still want a career in music outside the Church.

When my grandparents and uncles were alive I used to go to Jamaica sometimes and I found I was performing constantly. Jamaica is like a university for music – if you have talent you'll be spotted and given a break. It's a land where travellers go and never come back because they fall in love with the climate and people. If I didn't have ties here and I could afford the fare, I'd go back to Jamaica and start a band or open a club. I could easily get work as a singer there. But whether I earn a living from singing or not I'll always be a singer because singing is so much part of my soul that if you took it away from me I'd have no reason to live.

OCTOBER '07

Photograph: St Paul's Carnival, 2007

The artists

CLAUDIA AURORA

Claudia was born in Vila Nova de Gaia, near Oporto in Portugal and now lives in Bristol. She has been influenced by Brazilian culture since childhood and has trained in Brazil twice. She sings and dances with Afro-Brazilian and Cuban bands, Orchesta Montpelier and Grupo Ilu Axe, and teaches samba Baiano, samba reggae, afrobloco and samba no pe. She has recently discovered a talent for singing her native fado and performs at various venues in Bristol and throughout the UK.
www.claudia-aurora.com

PENNY AVERY

Penny is a dancer who was born in England to Jamaican parents. She specialises in west African dance and has trained with various dance teachers in Britain as well in Senegal. She has recently completed a three-year HND course in Contemporary Dance in Bristol and has formed an African-Contemporary dance company, Tolo ko Tolo, with Denise Rowe. She teaches and performs throughout the region and is working towards a degree in contemporary dance at Swansea University.
pennyjaav@yahoo.co.uk
www.tribeofdoris.co.uk

SONAL BAROT

Sonal is a classical Indian dancer who trained in the South Indian Bharata Natyam dance tradition both in India and the UK. Her teachers have included Kiran Ratna and Megan Lloyd at India Dance Wales; Meena Raman and Shri B. Seetharama Sarma in Chennai; and Mavin Khoo in London. She was born and lives in Bristol, and teaches and performs mainly for India Dance Wales at venues in England and Wales.
www.indiadancewales.com

RACHEL DE GARANG

Rachel was born in Bor in Southern Sudan and now lives in Bristol. She performs and teaches both traditional African and African-fusion dance – with influences from east, west and north Africa as well as Brazil – at Tribe of Doris and venues throughout the South West. She is currently studying for a degree in dance at Bath Spa University.
racheldegarang@planetwave.net
www.tribeofdoris.co.uk

DR JOEL

Dr Joel is a lyricist, composer, performer and educator from India's top rhythm academy, Sri JGTV Academy, Chennai. He has led participatory konnakol vocal percussion sessions for primary and secondary schools, youth groups, seniors, music academies and festivals. He has performed at major venues across the world and leads the trio JG Laya, featuring Subash Chandran ('king of konnakol') and Vikku Vinayakram. His exploratory collaborations have been with Billy Cobham, Airto Moreira, Dr Balamuralikrishna, Kula Shaker, Tinariwen and Seckou Keita. He has recently been approached by the viola star Rivka Golani to compose a concerto for viola and konnakol. He lives near Bath.
www.drjoelmusic.com
www.tribeofdoris.co.uk

CHARTWELL DUTIRO

Chartwell grew up in the predominantly Zezuru-speaking region of Zimbabwe where he played mbira for a Shona spiritual healer. He is now widely known as a master musician with a gift for bringing this sacred music and song to a wider audience through performance and teaching. He holds a MMus in ethnomusicology from SOAS (University of London) and has co-edited a book about his life and music, Zimbabwean Mbira Music on an International Stage (Ashgate, 2007). In 2005 he composed and performed mbira music for the Royal Shakespeare Company's production, 'Breakfast with Mugabe'. He has recorded several albums, both solo and with his band Spirit Talk Mbira. He currently lives in Devon.
cdutiro@yahoo.co.uk
www.tribeofdoris.co.uk

LOUIS ROGER EBOA

Louis Roger was born and brought up in Cameroon, where he trained with the dance company Beko's Stard. As a professional dancer he came to England in 2000 and settled first of all in London – where he performed in Patti Boulaye's Sun Dance and with the pan-African dance ensemble Azido – and then in Bristol. He teaches African-inspired dance to both adults and children, and trained children from four different schools for the COSTA (Commemoration of the Slave Trade Abolition) production, King Cotton, at Bristol's Colston Hall in October 2007.
louiroger@yahoo.fr

ALAIN HERNANDEZ CUNI

Alain was born in Havana where he trained as a traditional Cuban and folkloric dancer. He is a practising Santero or initiate into the Santería religion, which has its roots in the Yoruba spiritual system brought to Cuba by African slaves. He performs and teaches the dances of the Orishas (Santería deities) at Tribe of Doris and in Bristol. He also teaches salsa.
cubannights@hotmail.com
www.tribeofdoris.co.uk

SAMUEL HUTCHINSON

Samuel is a highly respected jazz, soul and reggae singer who has performed in Bristol and throughout the UK since the 1960s. He has sung with numerous bands including Jungle Red, the Panthers and the Tommy Hawkins band at the Locarno in central Bristol. He was born in Kingston, Jamaica, and now lives in Bristol.
www.stpaulscarnival.co.uk

BI DO IRIE

Bi Do is a percussionist and drum teacher who was born and brought up in Ivory Coast, West Africa. He began his professional career with Marie Rose Guiraud's company, Les Guirivoires, with whom he toured the world. He lived in Germany for ten years, where he formed and led the Ivorian band Zavoalo, before moving to Britain in 2003. He teaches and performs at Tribe of Doris and at various venues in and around Bristol, where he lives.
www.zavoalo.net
www.tribeofdoris.co.uk

CYRUS KHAJAVI

Cyrus was born and grew up in the Khorasan province of north-eastern Iran where the traditional music of many different tribes was part of everyday life. He came to England in 1974 to study architecture or engineering but instead became a musician. For six years he was a member of the internationally renowned rock band Quasar before reverting to his musical roots and forming the band Kooch, which is strongly influenced by the music Cyrus learned from his Azerbaijani mother. Cyrus holds a degree in music from Bath College of Higher Education, where he studied classical guitar and composition.
www.kooch.uk.com
tammy.khajavi@blueyonder.co.uk

EUGENIA LEDESMA

As a child growing up in Argentina, Eugenia performed with her father Victor Ledesma's traditional dance company. Their repertoire included Argentinian folk dances such as malambo, Argentinian samba and polka and Eugenia also learned to drum. When she was nineteen Eugenia came to England. She embarked on various jobs and training courses – carpentry, secretarial work, a degree in fine art at the University of the West of England – before establishing herself as a musician and dancer. She now sings with Bristol bands, Up, Bustle and Out and El Pato and teaches salsa locally and at Tribe of Doris.

montuno22@hotmail.com
www.tribeofdoris.co.uk

SONIA MUMTAZ

Sonia is an entirely self-taught Bollywood dancer who was born in England to Bangladeshi parents. In 2003 she was selected to be on the Channel 4 series 'Bollywood Star', a contest to find a British actor to take part in a Bollywood film. She and her sister, Mumtaz, subsequently started their own company, Bollywood Glamour, which performs at various venues in and around Bristol. Sonia teaches both adults and children in group classes and individually.

sonitastc@hotmail.com

CECILIA NDHLOVU

Cecilia grew up in Bulawayo in Matebeleland, southern Zimbabwe. She learned to dance at school where, because of her natural talent, she was known as 'magida omncane' (little dancer). When she was 16 Cecilia joined the women's dance troupe Black Umfolofi and several years later she started to sing and dance with the well known Zimbabwean musician Oliver Mtukudzi. She was with Mtukudzi's band for eight years during which time they toured extensively, but when one of their songs was considered anti-Mugabe and banned by the authorities, Cecilia, fearing for her safety, fled Zimbabwe. She now lives in Bristol and is a singer, drummer, dance performer and dance teacher.

agathapulu@yahoo.co.uk
www.tribeofdoris.co.uk

EURIDICE OYAGA DE HOLLIS

Euridice was born and grew up in Bogotá, Colombia. When she was a girl her grandmother taught her the traditional songs and dances of the Caribbean coastal region of Colombia, where she herself grew up. As a teenager Euridice toured throughout Europe, singing and dancing with her mother the well-known cantadora Totó de Momposina. Euridice now lives in Bath where she has her own dance company, Colores de mi Tierra, which features, alongside other Colombian musicians and dancers, three of her children. Euridice teaches Colombian dance in Bath and at Tribe of Doris.

admin@astarmusic.co.uk
www.tribeofdoris.co.uk

AYODELE SCOTT

Ayo was born in Freetown, Sierra Leone and came to England in 1987. He is highly respected as an African drum and dance teacher throughout the UK and regularly performs with the Afro-Celtic band Baka Beyond. He is currently working on Sameboat project, which is 'a ritual redemptive retracing of the Atlantic slave triangle'. The project was conceived in 2007, the bicentenary of the abolition of the slave trade, and the boat will sail in 2008.

www.sameboatproject.com
www.tribeofdoris.co.uk

ALPHONSE DAUDET TOUNA

Alphonse was born in Cameroon and now lives in Bristol. He is a musician, composer, instrument-maker and teacher. He founded and leads the Afro-Jazz band Hélélé, and is widely respected for his work in the local community – running workshops in prisons for young offenders; working with special needs groups; teaching children of all ages to sing, dance and play African percussion. In 2007 he ran a series of workshops at Bristol's Empire and Commonwealth Museum, teaching children about the Slave Trade as part of the COSTA Project (Commemoration of the Slave Trade Abolition) which culminated in the stage extravaganza King Cotton, at Bristol's Colston Hall.

www.myspace.com/helele
www.tribeofdoris.co.uk

SHELOK TSERING

Shelok was born and grew up in India where her parents fled when China invaded Tibet. Like many other Tibetans growing up in exile, Shelok has never seen her native land. She learned about Tibetan history and culture at the Tibetan Village Children's School in Dharamsala, and now she and her husband Dawa campaign to keep that culture alive amongst Tibetan exile communities throughout the world. In Britain they run workshops on Tibetan culture – including religion, cooking, singing and dancing – in order raise consciousness about their country and the plight of their people. Shelok is a talented singer and dancer and often performs her native songs at Tibetan Awareness events. She lives in Devon.
sheloktsering@hotmail.co.uk

ALEJANDRA VELASCO

Alejandra is a flamenco dancer and dance teacher. She was born and grew up in Madrid and holds a degree in Spanish Dance from the Real Consevatorio Profesional de Danza de Madrid. Her teacher for most of her training was Maria del Carmen Romero. Alejandra performs regularly throughout the UK and teaches group classes as well as individuals in both Cardiff and Bristol. She lives in Cardiff.
a.velasco@yahoo.es

ZDZISŁAWA (SYLVIA) ŻUKOWSKA

Sylvia was born in Italy to Polish parents who were war refugees. After the war her family came to England where they went from one displaced persons' camp to another. She and her husband now live in Trowbridge amongst a large Polish community, which in 1960 founded its own traditional Polish dance company, Kujawy. Sylvia joined Kujawy in 1966 and now performs with them at festivals and community events.
z.zukowska@talktalk.net

BINTA SUSO (front cover)

Binta is a singer who was born into a griot family of hereditary musicians in Gambia. In 2003, based in Bristol, she toured the UK with the band Jalikunda. Soon afterwards she embarked on an international exchange study programme at the Sund Folk College in Norway. She now performs with the Seckou Keita Quartet, with whom she recorded the album Afro-Mandinka Soul. She has recently settled in Nottingham.
www.seckoukeita.com

Links

Bristol Refugee Week • www.bristolrefugeeweek.co.uk
Bristol Refugee Week (Big Fun Day) • www.bristolrefugeeweek.co.uk/events
Bristol Asian Festival • www.bbc.co.uk/bristolasianfestival
Bristol Dance Centre • www.bristolcommunitydancecentre.co.uk
Bristol Harbour Festival • www.bristol.gov.uk/harbourfestival
Bristol Refugee Action • www.refugee-action.org.uk/bristol
Free Tibet Campaign • www.freetibet.org
Gathering Voices • www.gatheringvoices.org.uk
India Dance Wales • www.indiadancewales.com
Kuumba Arts and Community Resource Centre • www.kuumba.org.uk
Pierian Centre • www.pierian.co.uk
St Paul's Carnival • www.stpaulscarnival.co.uk
Tribe of Doris Intercultural Summer School • www.tribeofdoris.co.uk